Blow the Trumpet in Zion

by

Richard Booker

VICTORY HOUSE PUBLISHERS

Tulsa, Oklahoma

Scriptural quotations have been carefully selected from the following versions of the Bible:

King James Version (KJV)

The New King James Bible, copyright © 1982, Thomas Nelson Inc., Nashville, Tn. (NKJ)

The Living Bible, copyright © 1971, Tyndale House Publishers, Wheaton, Il. Used by permission. (TLB)

Revised Standard Version, copyright © 1973. (RSV)

Acknowledgements

My love and gratitude to the following:

My wife, Peggy, for typing the manuscript and sharing her life with me in Messiah Jesus.

The Jews, as the people chosen by God to be a blessing to the whole world.

Our dear friends at "The Word" Sunday School class in Dallas, Texas for their ministry of helps that made this book possible.

About the Author

Richard Booker is an author and Bible teacher presently living in Houston, Texas. His organization, Sounds of the Trumpet, Inc., provides Christian teachings through books, tapes, seminars etc. Prior to his call to the teaching ministry, Richard was a computer and management consultant climbing the corporate career ladder. His B.S. and M.B.A. degrees well prepared him. His career became his god, and he spent ten years chasing that illusory idol, dragging his wife, Peggy, across the country with him.

During that time he lectured in the United States, Canada and Mexico training over 1,000 management and computer personnel. His more than twenty articles appeared in the leading computer publications. He was listed in Who's Who in Computers and Automation, Who's Who in Training and Development, and The Dictionary of International Biography and was a frequent speaker for the American Management Association.

In the middle 1970s, God gave Richard an "Emmaus Road" experience that changed his life. He left his career to devote all his time to writing and teaching about God's Word. He is the author of a number of books (see back of book for details), articles for Christian magazines and other works.

In addition to his Bible classes and teaching tapes, Richard developed a one-day workshop called *Come and Dine* in which he teaches the principles of personal Bible study.

Contents

vi

1

All Eyes on Israel

It seems that every time I turn on the television they're talking about Israel and the Middle East. It's the same when I read the paper or pick up a magazine. The headlines are all about people and countries that seem a world far away and in which I've never had much interest before.

Yet, I find their names are becoming household words. Who hasn't heard of Menachem Begin, Anwar Sadat, the PLO and Yasser Arafat! Everybody's talking about them. They're the subject of conversation from California to Florida, Texas to Alaska, the White House to the school house and the United Nations to the neighborhood social. Why even the other day, the lady who works at the post office expressed concern over the Middle East. And so has the whole world.

All the world is watching Israel to see what they're going to do next. This tiny land, hardly the size of the state of

1

Indiana, U.S.A., with a population of only about three million, has captured the attention of the world.

All eyes are on Israel and the Middle East. The politicians are frantically seeking a diplomatic solution to the problems in that part of the world. The military leaders are preparing their war machines just in case the politicians fail. The economic stability of practically every nation in the world has become more and more dependent on and influenced by the situation in the oil-rich Middle East. The whole world is holding its breath while waiting for the next crisis to develop. As the Hebrew prophet Zechariah predicted, Jerusalem has become a heavy stone burdening the whole world (Zechariah 12:3).

Why is all of this happening? *Is there any explanation or is the present Middle East crisis just another passing coincidence of world history?* And how is it all going to end? Will Israel survive or will the Arabs drive them into the Mediterranean? Will the United States continue to support Israel or will we turn our back on Israel in favor of Arab oil? And what about Russia? Will they take over the world as they hope? Will there be a World War III or will we somehow find a way to live together in peace and ban the bomb?

Why I Wrote This Book

These are questions which concern us all. I believe I've found the answers in a book that too many of us have long overlooked. That book is the Holy Bible. That's right—the Bible!

As I've studied the Bible, I've discovered that God has a plan for this little nation of Israel. In examining this plan, any honest inquirer can see how God has been working it out in history. By comparing God's plan for Israel with the actual history of the Jews, it has become amazingly clear that the current crisis in the Middle East is not just a passing coincidence of world history. Instead, it is the final outworking of God's predetermined plan for the Hebrew people.

I'm sure you would like to know what this plan is and how

2

it might affect your life. I also want you to know. But even more importantly, God wants you to know. That's why I believe He is the One who put the desire in my heart to write this book.

I've written it for *four specific purposes*. First, to explain God's plan for Israel—as recorded in the Bible and worked out in history—so that you might understand it and respond to it positively in your life. Second, to inform Christians so as to encourage them to support the Jewish people with their prayers and works of lovingkindness. Third, it is a love gift from a Christian to the Jewish people, meant to give them hope in the dark days that lie ahead—and a calm assurance that if they will seek God with their whole heart they will find Him (Jeremiah 29:11-13). Finally, I wrote this book to promote greater understanding, care and love between Christians and Jews everywhere.

A Look At What's Ahead

You'll begin in chapter two by examining the incredible claim by the Jews that they are *God's chosen people*. Are they really God's chosen people, or is this just a myth invented by the Jews which they have somehow managed to perpetuate and use to their own advantage? And if they are God's chosen people—for what purpose did He choose them? Can it be that the Jews really were chosen by God as the people through which He would work out certain of His divine plans and purposes for planet earth? And if so, what should be our response?

Then in the next chapter, we'll look at an *ancient promise God gave to Abraham*. Long ago, God made a covenant with Abraham who was the father of the Jews. This covenant provided for certain blessings to Abraham and his descendants that were only partially fulfilled in the period of time covered by the Hebrew Scriptures (Old Testament part of the Bible). Their complete fulfillment was to take place in the latter days or end times of our present world order. *You will see in this chapter that current events in the Middle East are no passing coincidence of history but were foretold*

3

thousands of years ago by the Hebrew prophets, speaking under the inspiration of God. And the writers of the New Testament Scriptures are in perfect agreement with the Hebrew prophets concerning these events.

In chapter four, you'll follow the Hebrews from Abraham to Moses and read parts of a sermon preached by Moses thousands of years ago. In this sermon, Moses gave a *ten-part outline* of God's plan for Israel. As we study the Hebrew Scriptures and follow the trail of the Jewish people throughout history, we discover that he accurately predicted their past, present and future.

The chapters that follow (five to fourteen) provide a *survey of God's plan for Israel.* These chapters briefly describe how each of the ten parts of Moses' prediction have been fulfilled are being and will be fulfilled. As you follow the winding trail of this unfolding prophecy, you will begin to see that God has always been behind the scenes of history—moving world events to fulfill His ancient covenant with Abraham and the plan He has for Israel.

For the most part, the Jewish people feel like they don't have a friend in the whole world. History has demonstrated that Gentiles do not have a positive attitude towards the Jews, and, given the right moment and conditions, they might cause the Jews to suffer. The one exception should be Christians. Yet, Christians have not always shown compassion to the Jewish people. I believe that the relationship between Christians and Jews (particularly with the state of Israel) is going to be a major issue in the near future. We discuss this point in chapter fifteen by considering *"Why Christians should love Jews!"*

A great number of Jewish people are beginning to show more interest in their religious heritage. At the center of the Jewish faith is the teaching of the Messiah. The Hebrew Scriptures speak of a personal deliverer to be sent by God, who would rule Israel and the nations of the earth with justice and righteousness. He would usher in the golden age about which the prophets spoke. Chapter sixteen discusses the *Jewish Messiah* using the Hebrew Scriptures as the basis for recognizing Him.

In addition, there is a study guide at the end of each chapter to help you reinforce and highlight what you have learned in the chapter. The study guides may be completed on an individual or group basis.

The following page provides a chart entitled, *"God's Plan For Israel."* This chart is an outline of the information that you will be reading in this book through chapter fourteen. We will be referring to it from time to time. It would be helpful if you took a minute to look over the chart and familiarize yourself with it before reading the next chapter. It's worth noting that all the biblical references on the chart are from the Hebrew Scriptures.

In considering God's plan for Israel, it is obvious that God took the initiative to bring about some of the events while the Jewish people themselves caused some of them by their sin. Yet in His foreknowledge, God predicted through Moses and the prophets how the Jewish people would respond.

GOD'S PLAN FOR ISRAEL

A. GOD CHOOSES A PEOPLE
(DT.7:6-8;9:4-6;10:12-16)

1. TO WRITE AND PRESERVE THE SCRIPTURES
(EX.24:4-8;34:27-28)

2. TO REVEAL THE CHARACTER OF GOD
(EX.19:5; LEV.11:44-45;19:1-2)

3. TO BRING MESSIAH INTO THE WORLD
(GEN.22:18)

B. GOD'S COVENANT WITH ABRAHAM
(GEN.12:1-3,7;13:14-17;15:5,7,18;17:2,4-8)

1. TYPE OF COVENANT

   A. BINDING

   B. UNCONDITIONAL

   C. EVERLASTING

   D. LITERAL

2. COVENANT PROVISIONS

   A. LAND (GEN.15:18; NUM.34:1-12; JOS.1:1-4;
   EZ.47:15-20)

   B. NATION (GEN.17:18-19;22:17;28:13-14;35:10-12;
   49:9-10; 2SAM.7:12-13,16)

   C. BLESSING (GEN.22:18; JER.31:31-34; ZEC.12:8-10;
   13:1,8-9)

C. GOD'S PLAN FOR ISRAEL
(DT.4:23-31;30:1-6)

1. JEWS WILL BREAK THE COVENANT
(IS.57:5-8; JER.35:15; EZ.14:3-8; HOS.13:2-3)

2. GOD WILL DRIVE THEM FROM THEIR LAND
(LEV.26:25,30-32; DT.11:16-17; 28:25; IS.7:17-20;
JER.16:10-13)

3. GOD WILL SCATTER THEM AMONG THE NATIONS
(LEV.26:33,36-39; DT.28:25,64-67; HOS.9:17; AM.7:17)

4. JEWS WILL BE FEW IN NUMBER AMONG THE NATIONS
(DT.28:62-64; IS.10:22; EZ.6:8;12:15-16;20:37-38)

5. JEWS WILL SERVE OTHER GODS
(DT.28:64; JER.16:13; EZ.20:32-38)

6. GOD WILL PRESERVE A REMNANT
(LEV.26:36-39,44; IS.11:11-12; JER.30:10-11; EZ.12:16)

7. GOD WILL BRING THE JEWS BACK TO THEIR LAND
(JER.30:10-11; EZ.11:16-17; AM.9:14-15; ZEPH.3:20)

8. JEWS WILL GO THROUGH TRIBULATION
(JER.30:7; DAN.7:25;12:1; ZEC.13:8,14:1-2)

9. JEWS WILL RETURN TO GOD
(JER.24:7; EZ.11:17-20; HOS.3:4-5; ZEC.12:8-10:13:1)

10. GOD WILL REMEMBER HIS COVENANT
(LEV.26:40-46; IS.49:14-16; JER.33:14-17; EZ.16:62-63

2

God Chooses A People

We now seek to answer the question, *"Are the Jews God's chosen people?"* As a Christian, I must turn to the pages of the Bible for the answer. The Scriptures clearly declare with a loud voice that God did choose the Jews as the people through which He would work out certain of His divine plans and purposes for planet earth. You may not like God's selection, but you are stuck with it. You might as well get used to the idea and agree with God that He knows what He's doing and can choose anybody He desires for whatever His purposes.

The Chosen People

We find God's selection of the Jews revealed in the very first book of the Bible. The writer of *Genesis* tells us how God took the initiative to call Abram (Abraham) to be the human father of the Jews (Genesis 12:1-3). At that time,

God made a covenant with Abraham that bound Him forever to Abraham and his descendants. We'll consider this agreement in more detail in the next chapter.

God then confirmed His choice to Moses in the book of *Exodus.* This first took place when God appeared to Moses in a burning bush. Moses noticed that the bush was not consumed by the flame. His curiousity got the best of him. As he drew near to inspect the bush, God spoke these words to Moses, ". . . I am the God of your father—the God of Abraham, the God of Isaac, and the God of Jacob . . . I have surely seen the oppression of My people who are in Egypt, and have heard their cry because of their taskmasters, for I know their sorrows . . . Come now, therefore, and I will send you to Pharaoh that you may bring My people, the children of Israel, out of Egypt" (Exodus 3:6-10 NKJ).

Notice that God spoke of the Jews as His people. Moses then went to Pharaoh and demanded that he let "God's people" go. But Pharaoh didn't know that the Jews were God's people. Instead of letting them go, he made life even harder for them. Moses became discouraged by this negative turn of events. He quizzed God about the situation and why He hadn't caused Pharaoh to let "His people" go (Exodus 5:23).

God reassured Moses that He had heard him correctly and that the Jews really were His people. He again said to Moses concerning the Jews, "I will take you as My people, and I will be your God . . ." (Exodus 6:7 NKJ). With this added assurance that God was on his side, Moses again confronted Pharaoh and, with God's help, successfully lead the Jews out of Egypt.

In the third book of the Bible (*Leviticus*) we find God giving the Jews the religious system through which they were to approach Him. It was a system that set the Jews apart from their pagan neighbors. *Through this system, God would show the Jews that He had chosen them out of all the people of the earth to be used for certain of His divine plans and purposes.* He then reminded them of their special place in history with these words, " . . . I am the Lord

8

your God, who has separated you from the peoples . . . And you shall be holy (separate) to Me, for I the LORD am holy, and have separated you from the peoples, that you should be Mine" (Leviticus 20:24-26 NKJ).

In the book of *Numbers*, God directed the high priest to pronounce divine blessings on the Jews. He says, "The LORD bless you and keep you; The LORD make His face shine upon you, And be gracious to you; the LORD lift up His countenance upon you, And give you peace" (Numbers 6:24-26 NKJ).

Later in that same book of Numbers, King Balak (a Moabite) hired a false prophet by the name of Balaam for the purpose of pronouncing a curse on the Jews. But each time Balaam opened his mouth to curse them, God made him speak blessings instead. This happened four times. (See Numbers 22-24).

Balaam realized what was happening and said, "God is not a man, that He should lie, nor a son of man, that He should repent. Has He said, and will He not do it? Or has He spoken, and will He not make it good? Behold, I have received a commandment to bless; He has blessed, and I cannot reverse it" (Numbers 23:19-20 NKJ).

Balaam realized that God had purposed to bless the Jews, and there was nothing he could do to change the situation. Finally, he gave up trying to curse them. We see what God has blessed, no man can curse.

We also find in the book of *Deuteronomy* that the Jews have been chosen by God. He says to them in Deuteronomy 7:6, "For you are a holy people to the LORD your God; the LORD your God has chosen you to be a people for Himself, a special treasure above all the peoples on the face of the earth" (NKJ).

God then repeats His divine selection of the Jews in Deuteronomy 14:2, "For you are a holy people to the LORD your God, and the LORD has chosen you to be a people for Himself, a special treasure above all the peoples who are on the face of the earth" (NKJ).

Acknowledged In The Psalms

As we continue in the Hebrew Scriptures, we find numerous references to the belief that the Jews are God's chosen people. Here are a few in the book of *Psalms:*

"Blessed is the nation whose God is the LORD, and the people whom He has chosen as His own inheritance" (Psalm 33:12 NKJ).

"O seed of Abraham His servant, You children of Jacob, His chosen ones" (Psalm 105:6 NKJ).

"Remember me, O LORD, with the favor You have toward Your people; Oh, visit me with Your salvation, That I may see the benefit of Your chosen ones, That I may rejoice in the gladness of Your nation, That I may glory with Your inheritance" (Psalm 106:4-5 NKJ).

"For the LORD has chosen Zion; He has desired it for His habitation: This is My resting place forever; Here I will dwell, for I have desired it" (Psalm 132:13-14 NKJ).

"For the LORD has chosen Jacob for Himself, Israel for His special treasure" (Psalm 135:4 NKJ).

Proclaimed By The Prophets

The *prophets* picked up this theme and often used it as a means to encourage the Jewish people during difficult times and to praise God in times of blessings. The one thing they were sure of was that *God had chosen them and would never forsake them no matter how hopeless their situation seemed.* Here are some of their words:

"But you, Israel, are My servant, Jacob, whom I have chosen, the descendants of Abraham My friend. . .'You are My servant, I have chosen you and have not cast you away' " (Isaiah 41:8-9 NKJ).

"But now, thus says the LORD, who created you, O Jacob, And He who formed you, O Israel: 'Fear not, for I have redeemed you; I have called you by your name; You are Mine' " (Isaiah 43:1 NKJ).

"This people I have formed for Myself; They shall declare My praise" (Isaiah 43:21 NKJ).

"Yet hear now, O Jacob My servant, And Israel whom I have chosen" (Isaiah 44:1 NKJ).

"Have you not considered what these people have spoken, saying, 'The two families which the LORD has chosen, (Israel and Judah), He has also cast them off'? Thus they have despised My people, as if they should no more be a nation before them. Thus says the LORD: 'If My covenant is not with day and night, and if I have not appointed the ordinances of heaven and earth, then I will cast away the descendants of David My servant, so that I will not take any of his descendants to be rulers over the descendants of Abraham, Isaac, and Jacob. For I will cause their captives to return, and will have mercy on them' " (Jeremiah 33:24-26 NKJ).

"Nevertheless I will remember My covenant with you in the days of your youth, and I will establish an everlasting covenant with you. . .And I will establish My covenant with you. Then you shall know that I am the LORD" (Ezekiel 16:60, 62 NKJ).

"You only have I known of all the families of the earth . . ." (Amos 3:2 NKJ).

Confirmed By Paul

This same theme continues in the *New Testament Scriptures*. The apostle Paul, a Jew himself, wrote the following about his brethren after the flesh:

"God has given you so much, but you still will not listen to him. He took you as his own special chosen people and led you along with a bright cloud of glory and told you how very much he wanted to bless you. He gave you his rules for daily life so you would know what he wanted you to do. He let you worship him, and gave you mighty promises" (Romans 9:4 TLB).

11

"I ask then, has God rejected and deserted his people the Jews? Oh no, not at all. Remember that I myself am a Jew, a descendant of Abraham and a member of Benjamin's family. No, God has not discarded his own people whom he chose from the very beginning. . . .For God's gifts and his call can never be withdrawn; he will never go back on his promises" (Romans 11:1-2, 29 TLB).

In these and many other Scriptures, the Bible clearly states that God chose the Jews as the people through which He would work out certain of His divine plans and purposes. We now want to answer the question, *"What are these divine plans and purposes?"*

Why God Chose The Jews
To appreciate why God chose the Jews, it is helpful to understand why God made us in the first place. Only God would have the answer to such a profound question. And He tells us in the Bible. God said through the prophet Jeremiah that He created us so that we might know Him and fellowship with Him forever (Jeremiah 9:23-24). The biblical use of the word "know" means to have a personal intimacy with Him and enjoy His company into eternity.

Yet, in the book of Genesis, we learn that man sinned by disobeying God. The result of this sin was that man was no longer able to fellowship with God, and over the years his understanding of God became perverted. Man lost that intimate relationship with his Creator. (See Genesis 3.)

As man drifted further from God, all the world became very evil. God could see that man would never turn from his wicked ways. In view of this, God decided to destroy all of humanity with a great flood and start all over again with the one righteous man He could find. This was a man named Noah (Genesis 6:5-8). Because Noah walked with God, the Lord spared Noah and his family bringing them safely through the flood.

This judgement by God brought man back to Him for

awhile. Noah and his sons, Shem, Ham and Japeth, along with their families, continued to worship God. But as other generations were born, they gradually began to drift back into idolatry and immorality. It took about 500 years from the flood for the whole earth to once again turn its back on God.

Even though God must have been saddened by the way man was living, He did not give up on mankind. He had a plan for drawing man back to himself. *This plan centered around a Chaldean (Babylonian) man by the name of Abram (later Abraham).*

Abraham was a descendant of Shem. His family worshiped idols (Joshua 24:2). They lived in the city of Ur, located in Babylon between the Tigris and Euphrates Rivers. Babylon was a very sophisticated, culturally advanced country. But it was a pagan one, as well. The people worshipped the moon and made idols of a moon goddess.

God, for His own sovereign purposes, called Abraham out of this environment. He told Abraham to leave his pagan land, idols and household and go to a new land that God would show him. Abraham heard the voice of God and obeyed it. *This begins the history of God's chosen people, Israel.*

Chosen for What?

God chose Abraham and his descendants as the human vessels through which He would reveal Himself to the world. They were to be God's human showroom displaying His character to a world that had once again lost touch with Him.

The Hebrews were to fulfill this call in three ways. *First, they were to write down and preserve God's revelation of Himself to mankind* (2 Peter 1:20-21). They faithfully did this by recording and protecting the Word of God, which eventually became known as "the Bible." No other book in man's history has been more accurately and reliably preserved than the Bible. By studying the Bible, we can have a correct understanding of God and come to know Him and

13

fellowship with Him as He originally intended us to do. Through the Jewish writers, God was going to reveal Himself to the world by a book.

But a book can only do so much. People need more than just words. So *the second way the Jews were to reveal the truth about God to the world was through their holy lives.* The word holy means "separate" or different. God was different from the view the pagan world had of Him. But how could He show them He was different? How could He show them what He was like? He chose to show them through the Hebrew nation. God would do this through the moral, religious and civil laws that He would give them. As the Jews lived in obedience to these laws, they would be a light to the darkened pagan world showing them the one true God and what He was really like. (See Exodus 19:5; Leviticus 11:44-45; 19:1-2.) Through Abraham and his descendants, God was going to reveal Himself to the world by a nation of people who had been no people.

The third way the Jews would fulfill their divine call was by bringing the Messiah (Savior) into the world. You see, the Jews didn't always do that good of a job showing their pagan neighbors what God was like. They didn't always trust and obey Him. Sometimes their light was very dim. God needed a more reliable witness to His existence, greatness and moral character. He decided to come into the world Himself as a human being in order to be the perfect revelation to the world of what He is like. God chose the Jews as the ethnic people through which He would be born. He would be God in the flesh living among His people as the supreme witness to His own heart and character. Through the Messiah (Savior), God was going to show the world what He was like in the person of His Son—Jesus of Nazareth.

The New Testament Scriptures present Jesus as the perfect revelation of the unseen God. Jesus Himself said, "And he who sees Me sees Him who sent Me" (John 12:45 NKJ).

One of Jesus' disciples by the name of Philip said to Jesus, "Lord, show us the Father, and it is sufficient for us." Jesus said to him, "Have I been with you so long and yet you have not known Me, Philip? He who has seen Me has seen the Father. . . " (John 14:8-9 NKJ).

John wrote about Jesus, "No one has seen God at any time. The only begotten Son, who is in the bosom of the Father, He has declared Him" (John 1:18 NKJ).

Paul wrote in Colossians 1:15 that Jesus is the "image of the invisible God." The writer of Hebrews says that Jesus "bears the very stamp of God's nature" (Hebrews 1:3).

These phrases refer to an engraving on a coin. The engraving came from a stamp which was used to make the impression on the coin. Unless you work in the mint where the coin is made, you have never seen the stamp. But you can know exactly what it looks like by looking at the coin.

Likewise, no one has ever seen God. But we can know exactly what He is like in His personal and moral being by looking at Jesus Christ, the Jewish Messiah and Savior of the world.

So in case you've ever wondered, the Bible makes it very clear that the Jews are God's chosen people. God carved a people out of the human race for the purpose of using them as a means for revealing himself to the world. He did not do this because the Jews were superior to the Gentiles (Deuteronomy 7:6-8; 9:4-6; 10:12-16). In fact, there was no such person as a Jew before God called them into existence. God chose Abraham and his descendants simply because that was what He wanted to do. As the sovereign God of the universe, it was His plan and good pleasure to make himself known in this way. *And it all began with God's ancient covenant with Abraham.*

Chapter 2—God Chooses A People

Study Guide 1

1. Write out three Scriptures that tell us the Jews are God's chosen people.

   a. _Psalms 106 Remember me as you remember Isreal_

   b. _Isiah 414 Isreal who I have chosen._

   c. _Isah 41 8-9 Chosen_

2. List and explain the three ways the Jews were to fulfill their divine call.

   a. _Bible - keep up scriptures_

   b. _Life - lie life apart from idols_

   c. _Jesus - be the race_

3

God's Covenant With Abraham

It is often said that the "key to the future lies in the past." What is meant by this is that we can better understand what is happening around us now, and what is going to happen in the future, if we understand what has happened in the past. This is particularly true in regard to the current crises in the Middle East and where it is leading us to.

Indeed, the key to understanding today's headlines and tomorrow's news lies in the past within the sacred covenant God made with Abraham. We're now going to examine this covenant through the pages of the Bible, using it as the key for understanding current and future events.

The Abrahamic Covenant

When God called Abraham, He entered into a *covenant* with him. The covenant ceremony is described in Genesis 15. The type of covenant that God made with Abraham was

17

a blood covenant. A blood covenant was the most binding, the most solemn and the most sacred of all compacts. *It was a literal, unconditional, everlasting covenant that absolutely could not be broken.*

This was a literal covenant in that God meant to do just what He said. It was unconditional in that its fulfillment depended entirely on God. Later, God made it known that the covenant blessings were conditional based on the Jewish people's obedience to the covenant. But the covenant itself was unconditional based on God's faithfulness and Abraham's belief. Finally, the covenant was everlasting in that God said it would stand forever.

Abraham's part was to believe. And because Abraham believed, God swore by himself to guarantee the fulfillment of the covenant (Genesis 22:16). This explains why God has always kept alive a remnant of Abraham's descendant's even though they have not always honored God's covenant with them through their father Abraham. The covenant was actually between God and Abraham, yet Abraham's descendants would be blessed because of it.

Here now is the basic covenant God made with Abraham. Genesis reads, "Now the LORD has said to Abram: Get out of your country, From your kindred and from your father's house; To a land that I will show you. I will make you a great nation; I will bless you And make your name great; and you shall be a blessing. I will bless those who bless you, And I will curse him who curses you; And in you all the families of the earth shall be blessed' " (Genesis 12:1-3 NKJ).

The Bible says that Abraham believed God (Genesis 15:6) and journeyed to this new land God had promised him. Once he got there, God confirmed His covenant with Abraham and gave him some *additional details.* God further explained to Abraham:

". . .To your descendants I will give this land" (Genesis 12:7 NKJ).

". . .Lift your eyes now and look from the place where you are——northward, southward, eastward and west-

18

ward; for all the land which you see I give to you forever. And I will make your descendants as the dust of the earth; so that if a man could number the dust of the earth, then your descendants also could be numbered. Arise, walk in the land through its length and its width, for I give it to you" (Genesis 13:14-17 NKJ).

" '. . .Look now toward heaven, and count the stars if you are able to number them. . . So shall your descendants be. . . I am the LORD, who brought you out of Ur of the Chaldeans, to give you this land to inherit it'. . . On the same day the LORD made a covenant with Abram, saying: 'To your descendants I have given this land, from the river of Egypt to the great river, the River Euphrates-' " (Genesis 15:5,7,18 NKJ).

"And I will make My covenant between Me and you, and will multiply you exceedingly. . . As for Me, behold, My covenant is with you, and you shall be a father of many nations. No longer shall your name be called Abram, but your name shall be Abraham; for I have made you a father of many nations. I will make you exceedingly fruitful; and I will make nations of you, and kings shall come from you. And I will establish My covenant between Me and you and your descendants after you in their generation, For an everlasting covenant, to be God to you and your descendants after you. Also I give to you and your descendants after you the land in which you are a stranger, all the land of Canaan, as an everlasting possession; and I will be their God" (Genesis 17:2,4-8 NKJ).

"In blessing I will bless you, and in multiplying I will multiply your descendants as the stars of the heaven and as the sand which is on the seashore; and your descendants shall possess the gate of their enemies. In your seed all the nations of the earth shall be blessed. . ." (Genesis 22:17-18 NKJ).

The Covenant Perpetuated

As God gave Abraham these details about the covenant, we see that He assured Abraham that *He would continue the covenant with Abraham's descendants.* Abraham's descendants were not always true to the covenant. This naturally made them feel guilty and think that perhaps God would forsake them. For this reason, God found it necessary to frequently remind the Jewish people of the binding, literal, unconditional, everlasting nature of the covenant. His reminders are too numerous to list, but here are a few:

"He has remembered His covenant forever, the word which He commanded for a thousand generations, the covenant which He made with Abraham, And His oath to Isaac, And confirmed it to Jacob for a statute, To Israel for an everlasting covenant" (1 Chronicles 16:15-17 NKJ).

"Incline your ear, and come to Me. Hear, and your soul shall live; And I will make an everlasting covenant with you——" (Isaiah 55:3 NKJ).

". . .I will make an everlasting covenant with them" (Isaiah 61:8 NKJ).

"And I will make an everlasting covenant with them, that I will not turn away from doing them good; but I will put My fear in their hearts so that they will not depart from Me" (Jeremiah 32:40 NKJ).

". . .I will deal with you as you have done, who despised the oath by breaking the covenant. Nevertheless I will remember my covenant with you in the days of your youth, and I will establish an everlasting covenant with you" (Ezekiel 16:59-60 NKJ).

"Moreover I will make a covenant of peace with them, and it shall be an everlasting covenant with them. . ." (Ezekiel 37:26 NKJ).

In the New Testament Scriptures, Paul adds,

"For the gifts and the calling of God are irrevocable" (Romans 11:29 NKJ).

All these references tell us very clearly this is an unconditional covenant based on what God would do for the Jews because of their father Abraham. *Although the blessings of the covenant are conditional, the covenant itself is eternal.* Leviticus 26 and Deuteronomy 28 provide a good overview of the general blessings for obedience and judgements for disobedience. As these two chapters provide a broad sweep of Jewish history, I recommend you read them in their entirety.

The Covenant Provisions

As we examine this covenant, we find it consists of *three major promises* that God made to Abraham. Specifically, God promised Abraham that He would make his descendants a *great nation*. Now a nation of people must have a land on which to live. So God also promised to give Abraham a *land* on which his descendants would live forever in peace with their neighbors. Finally, God promised Abraham that one would come from his loins who would be a *blessing* to the whole world. The "Coming One" was to be the Jewish *Messiah* who would also be the Savior of the world. When He came, He would make a new covenant through which spiritual blessings would come to both Jew and Gentile alike.

Because God made His covenant with Abraham, He decreed blessings on those who blessed Abraham and curses on those who cursed him. Of course, this included Abraham's descendants as well. Biblical accounts and modern history have substantiated this divine decree. All nations that have favored the Jews have been blessed by God. But nations that have opposed the Jews have fallen under God's judgement.

Throughout the Hebrew Scriptures, God amplifies and enlarges upon these three major covenant promises. The New Testament Scriptures continue the story giving even greater clarity concerning God's plan to fulfill these promises. We're now going to take a closer look at these three promises.

The Land Promise

God promised to Abraham and his descendants the land area that lies between the Mediterranean Sea and the Euphrates River. "On the same day the LORD made a covenant with Abram, saying: To your descendants I have given this land, from the river of Egypt to the great river, the River Euphrates" (Genesis 15:18 NKJ).

There is some question as to what is meant by the "river of Egypt." Some believe this refers to the Nile. However, other serious Bible students believe this may be referring to a dry river bed located in the Sinai called the Wadi-el-Arish.

The book of Numbers adds the following details concerning the borders of the promised land:

"The LORD told Moses to tell the people of Israel, 'When they come into the land of Canaan (I am giving you the entire land as your homeland), the southern portion of the country will be the wilderness of Zin, along the edge of Edom. The southern boundary will begin at the Dead Sea, and will continue south past Scorpion Pass in the direction of Zin. Its southernmost point will be Kadesh-barnea, from which it will go to Hazaraddar, and on to Azmon. From Azmon the boundary will follow the Wadi-el-Arish down to the Mediterranean Sea.

Your western boundary will be the coastline of the Mediterranean Sea.

Your northern border will begin at the Mediterranean Sea and will proceed eastward to Mount Hor, then to Lebo-Hamath, and on through Zedad and Ziphron to Hazar-enan.

The eastern border will be from Hazar-enan south to Shepham, then on the Riblah at the east side of Ain. From there it will make a large halfcircle, first going south and then westward until it touches the southernmost tip of the Sea of Galilee, and then along the Jordan River, ending at the Dead Sea' " (Numbers 34:1-12 TLB).

The prophet Ezekiel gives the following information:

"The northern boundary will run from the Mediterranean toward Hethlon, then on through Labweh to Zedad, then to Berothah and Sibraim, which are on the border between Damascus and Hamath, and finally to Hazer-hatticon, on the border of Hauran. So the northern border will be from the Mediterranean to Hazorenon, on the border with Hamath to the north and Damascus to the south.

The eastern border will run south from Hazar-enon to Mount Hauran, where it will bend westward to the Jordan at the southern tip of the Sea of Galilee, and down along the Jordan River separating Israel from Gilead, past the Dead Sea to Tamar.

The southern border will go west from Tamar to the springs at Meribath-kadesh and then follow the course of the brook of Egypt (Wadi-el-Arish) to the Mediterranean.

On the west side, the Mediterranean itself will be your boundary, from the southern boundary to the point where the northern boundary begins" (Ezekiel 47:15-20 TLB).

Historically, the Jews have never been in full control of all this land area which God promised them. In view of this, the ultimate fulfillment must come in the future. This land area which God will eventually give the Jews includes land which is now part of the nations of Lebanon, Syria, Jordan, and possibly Iraq. *This is what the fighting today in the Middle East is all about.*

It is possible that Israel will not get all of this land until the return of Messiah Jesus. But one thing is clear. God will allow Israel to expand its borders to get larger portions of it.

And the Arabs, who have provoked Israel to fight, will demand that Israel return the captured land. It is no coincidence that Israel has captured more land with each war it has had to fight since becoming a nation. Although it has had to give up some of the territory it has won, *Israel will eventually get it all.*

The Nation Promise

God promised Abraham that his descendants would become a great nation. The general promise is in Genesis 12:2 where God says, "I will make you a great nation; I will bless you and make your name great; And you shall be a blessing" (NKJ). God further adds, ". . .I will multiply your descendants as the stars of the heaven and as the sand which is on the seashore. . ." (Genesis 22:17 NKJ).

It is interesting that Abraham had no children at the time God made him this promise. His wife, Sarah, was too old to have children. Abraham thought he would help God fulfill this promise so he had a child by Hagar, Sarah's Egyptian handmaid. This child was named Ishmael. Ishmael became the father of the Arab nations, and it seems for this reason the Arabs claim title deed to the land called Palestine.

But this was not God's will. His promise was to bless *Abraham and Sarah's union.* God miraculously restored Sarah's body so that she conceived and bore Abraham a son named *Isaac.* Genesis 17:18-19 reads, "And Abraham said to God, 'Oh, that Ishmael might live before you!' " Then God said, "No, Sarah your wife shall bear you a son, and you shall call his name Isaac; I will establish My covenant with him for an everlasting covenant, and with his descendants after him" (NKJ).

Isaac married Rebekah who bore him two sons—Esau and Jacob. God chose to continue the covenant through *Jacob.* God said to Jacob, ". . . I am the LORD God of Abraham your father and the God of Isaac; the land on which you lie I will give it to you and your descendants. Also your descendants shall be as the dust of the earth; you shall spread abroad to the west and the east, to the north and the south; and in you and in your seed all the families of the earth shall be blessed" (Genesis 28:13-14 NKJ).

Later, God repeated His promise to Jacob and changed his name to Israel. Genesis 35:10-12 reads, "And God said to him (Jacob), 'Your name is Jacob; your name shall not be called Jacob anymore, but Israel shall be your name.' So He called his name Israel. Also God said to him: 'I am God Almighty. Be fruitful and multiply; a nation and a company of nations shall proceed from you, and kings shall come from your body. The land which I gave Abraham and Isaac I give to you; and to your descendants after you I give this land' " (NKJ).

Jacob had twelve sons who became the heads of the twelve tribes of Israel. Their names are Reuben, Simeon, Levi, Judah, Issachar, Zebulun, Gad, Asher, Dan, Naphtali, Joseph and Benjamin (Genesis 49:1-28). The nation of Israel began to come into existence from the offspring of these twelve sons.

Judah was chosen as the family line through which would come the kings of Israel (Genesis 49:10). One of these kings was to be greater than all the rest. He was to be the King of Kings who would make Israel the greater nation God had promised to Abraham.

One of Judah's descendants was King David (Genesis 38; Ruth 4:18-22). God chose *David* as the royal family through which He would confirm and fulfill His covenant to Abraham regarding the nation of Israel.

God spoke these words to David through the prophet Nathan:

"When your days are fulfilled and you rest with your fathers, I will set up your seed after you, who will come from your body, and I will establish his kingdom. He shall build a house for My name, and I will establish the throne of his kingdom forever. . . And your house and your kingdom shall be established forever before you. Your throne shall be established forever" (2 Samuel 7:12-13, 16 NKJ).

Now kings and royal families don't usually last very long. They either die or get killed. David is the one exception. God gave David a promise that has its roots in the Abrahamic covenant. It's a promise no other king of any nation has ever had. *God promised David that He would have a descendant who would rule over Jerusalem forever. The Jews recognized this promise to be fulfilled in the Messiah.*

God later confirmed this promise through the prophet Jeremiah:

"Yes, the day will come, says the Lord, when I will do for Israel and Judah all the good I promised them. At that time I will bring to the throne the true Son of David, and he shall rule justly. In that day the people of Judah and Jerusalem shall live in safety and their motto will be, 'The Lord is our righteousness!' For the Lord declares that from then on, David shall forever have an heir sitting on the throne of Israel. And there shall always be Levites to offer burnt offerings and meal offerings and sacrifices to the Lord.

Then this message came to Jeremiah from the Lord:

'If you can break my covenant with the day and with the night so that day and night don't come on their usual schedule, only then will my covenant with David, my servant, be broken so that he shall not have a son to reign upon his throne; and my covenant with the Levite priests, my ministers, is non-cancelable. And as the stars cannot be counted nor the sand upon the seashores measured, so the descendants of David my servant and the line of the Levites who minister to me will be multiplied.'

The Lord spoke to Jeremiah again and said:

'Have you heard what people are saying?—that the Lord chose Judah and Israel and then abandoned them! They are sneering and saying that Israel isn't worthy to be counted as a nation. But this is the Lord's reply: I would no more reject my people than I would reject my laws of night and day, of earth and sky. I will never abandon the Jews, or David my servant, or change the plan that his Child will someday rule these descendants of Abraham, Isaac and Jacob. Instead I will restore their prosperity and have mercy on them' " (Jeremiah 33:14-26 TLB).

Israel's sovereignty as a nation and David's dynasty ceased with the Babylonian captivity. But God's promise was eternal. So the Jews were looking for their Messiah who would come and deliver them from their enemies, establish the kingdom and rule from the throne of his father David. *The New Testament Scriptures identify Jesus as the greater Son of David.* In Luke, the angel Gabriel said to Mary, ". . .Do not be afraid, Mary, for you have found favor with God. And behold, you will conceive in your womb and bring forth a Son, and shall call His name Jesus. He will be great, and will be called the Son of the Highest; and the Lord God will give Him the throne of His father David. And He will reign over the house of Jacob forever, and of His kingdom there will be no end" (Luke 1:30-33 NKJ). *We learn from this birth announcement that Jesus was a descendant of King David.* The book of Matthew records the genealogy of Jesus through Joseph. Joseph was a descendant of David through his son Solomon. *Through Joseph, Jesus was the legal heir to the throne.* Luke preserves the record of Jesus' genealogy through Mary. Mary was a descendant of David through his son Nathan. *Through Mary, Jesus was in the blood line of David and the rightful heir to the throne.* If the Hebrews had not been under Roman rule Jesus would have been their king. Pilate was absolutely correct when he made a sign to put on Jesus' cross identifying Him as the "King of the Jews!" How tragic that the Jews as a nation did not accept Jesus as such. But one day they will.

It's helpful to know that the Jews kept very accurate genealogical records in their temple. Every Jew could identify and prove which tribe he belonged to. But in 70 AD, the Romans destroyed Jerusalem and the temple where these records were kept. The result was that after 70 AD, not one Jew could prove he was a descendant of David. His genealogy was destroyed. The point of this is that no Jew after 70 AD can rightfully claim the throne of David. *Jesus is the only Jew alive today who can prove He is in the line of David.* This is because the Bible is the only genealogical record we have today showing David's descendants.

So you see, whoever the Messiah was, He had to come before 70 AD. This is the only way his claim to be the Son of David could be verified. Jesus was the final king in the line of David. Since He never married and had children of His own, there can be no more after Him. He is the eternal Son of David and King of the Jews who will come again as King of Kings to establish Israel as the head nation of all nations in fulfillment of God's promise to Abraham.

The Blessing Promise

The third promise God made to Abraham was that he would be a blessing to all mankind through one of his descendants who would be the Jewish Messiah and Savior of the world. We again refer to Genesis 12:2 for the general promise from God, "I will make you a great nation; I will bless you And make your name great; And you will be a blessing" (NKJ).

In this verse, God makes a sweeping commitment to Abraham that he would be a blessing. God then confirms this promise and gives Abraham added insight. He says to Abraham, "In your seed all the nations of the earth shall be blessed. . ." (Genesis 22:18 NKJ). What a staggering promise! Notice the magnitude of it. *Abraham's seed will be a blessing to all nations of the earth. But how?*

As time went by, God raised up the prophet Jeremiah to explain how Abraham's seed would be a blessing to all mankind. God spoke these words through Jeremiah:

"Behold the days are coming, says the LORD, when I will make a new covenant with the house of Israel and with the house of Judah—

28

Not according to the covenant that I made with their fathers in the day I took them by the hand to bring them out of the land of Egypt, My covenant which they brake, though I was a husband to them, says the LORD.

But this is the covenant that I will make with the house of Israel: after these days, says the LORD, I will put My law in their minds, and write it in their hearts; and I will be their God, and they shall be my people.

No more shall every man teach his neighbor, and every man his brother, saying, 'Know the LORD,' for they all shall know Me, from the least of them to the greatest of them, says the LORD. For I will forgive their iniquity and their sin I will remember no more" (Jeremiah 31:31-34 NKJ).

Jeremiah and many other Old Testament prophets explain that this blessing was to be of a *spiritual nature*. It is concerned with the forgiveness of sin and the imparting of spiritual life. Jeremiah speaks of this as a *new covenant*. He calls it a new covenant because it would bring results that the law, which was part of the old covenant, could not produce. The law, particularly the Ten Commandments, cannot bring forgiveness of sin. Instead they condemn us because no one can keep them. But in the new covenant, God would bring foregiveness of sin through the Messiah. The Messiah would offer Himself as the innocent substitutionary sacrifice, not only for the sins of the Jews, but for Gentiles as well. And the Messiah would give God's very own Spirit to all who put their faith in Him. In this way, all could have their sins forgiven, all could receive eternal life and all could know God personally. This is how Abraham would be a blessing to the whole world.

The New Testament Scriptures present Jesus as the One who came to establish this new covenant. He made the announcement as He celebrated the passover meal with His disciples. Matthew gives us the following account: "And as they were eating, Jesus took bread, blessed it and broke it, and gave it to the disciples and said, 'Take, eat; this is my body.' Then He took the cup, and gave thanks, and gave it to them, saying, 'Drink from it, all of you. For this is My blood of the new covenant, which is shed for many for the remission of sins' " (Matthew 26:26-28 NKJ).

In these and many other verses, Jesus claimed that He was the long-awaited Messiah who had come to fulfill God's covenant promise to Abraham. Both Jew and Gentile alike would be saved by faith in Him. But the Jews as a nation rejected Jesus as their Messiah. Therefore they have temporarily missed the blessings of the covenant. Although the Jews rejected Jesus, the Gentiles—on an individual basis—accepted Him, so that the spiritual blessings of the Abrahamic covenant have come to them as they personally acknowledge Jesus as their Lord and Savior.

The apostle Paul explained it this way in his letter to the Galatians:

"And the Scripture, foreseeing that God would justify the nations by faith, preached the gospel to Abraham beforehand, saying, 'In you all the nations shall be blessed.' So then those who are of faith are blessed with believing Abraham. . . that the blessing of Abraham might come upon the Gentiles in Christ Jesus, that we might receive the promise of the Spirit through faith. . . Now to Abraham and his Seed were the promises made. He does not say, 'And to seeds,' as of many, but as of one, 'And to your Seed,' who is Christ. . . But the Scripture has confined all under sin, that the promise by faith in Christ Jesus might be given to those who believe. . . There is neither Jew nor Greek, there is neither slave nor free, there is neither male nor female; for you are all one in Christ Jesus. And if you are Christ's, then you are Abraham's seed, and heirs according to the promise" (Galatians 3:8-9,14,16,22,28-29 NKJ). (See also Ephesians 2:11-22.)

Jews Not Forsaken

We see from these and many other verses that God has made the new covenant blessings available to the Gentiles. *But this does not mean that God has forsaken the Jews.* He cannot forsake them because of the nature of the Abrahamic covenant. This is the heart of Paul's discussion in Romans 9-11. He says:

"Does this mean that God has rejected his Jewish people forever? Of course not! His purpose was to make his salvation available to the Gentiles and then the Jews would be jealous and begin to want God's salvation for themselves. Now if the whole world became rich as a result of God's offer of salvation, when the Jews stumbled over it and turned it down, think how much greater a blessing the world will share in later on when the Jews, too, come to Christ."

"I want you to know about this truth from God, dear brothers, so that you will not feel proud and start bragging. Yes, it is true that some of the Jews have set themselves against the Gospel now, but this will last only until all of you Gentiles come to Christ—those of you who will. And then all Israel will be saved. Do you remember what the prophets said about this? 'There shall come out of Zion a Deliverer, and he shall turn the Jews from all ungodliness. At that time I will take away their sins, just as I promised.'

Now many of the Jews are enemies of the Gospel. They hate it. But this has been a benefit to you, for it has resulted in God's giving his gifts to you Gentiles. Yet the Jews are still beloved of God because of his promises to Abraham, Isaac, and Jacob. For God's gifts and his call can never be withdrawn; he will never go back on his promises" (Romans 11:11-12, 25-29 TLB).

Israel And Jesus

The Jews as a nation will eventually acknowledge Jesus as their Messiah. They will once again turn their hearts to

31

God. The Bible says this will happen in the latter days after the Jews have returned to their land from many years of exile. Jeremiah spoke these words for God, "For I will set My eyes on them for good, and I will bring them back to this land; I will build them and not pull them down, and I will plant them and not pluck them up. Then I will give them a heart to know Me, that I am the LORD; and they shall be my people, and I will be their God, for they shall return to me with their whole heart" (Jeremiah 24:6-7 NKJ).

When the Jewish people as a nation return to God, *the veil on their spiritual eyes will be lifted so that they will recognize and accept Jesus as their Messiah.* They will then enter into the new covenant and receive the blessings that it offers. Again we learn from Jeremiah, "I will cleanse them from all their iniquity by which they have sinned against Me, and I will pardon all their iniquities by which they have sinned and by which they transgressed against Me" (Jeremiah 33:8 NKJ).

When this happens, the Jewish people as a nation will pray for Messiah Jesus to come to planet earth to be their king and save them from the threat of annihilation at the hands of the Gentile nations which will be gathered against them (Joel 3:1-2; Zechariah 12:2-3, 8-9).

Then shall be fulfilled the words of the prophet Zechariah:

"In that day the LORD will defend the inhabitants of Jerusalem; the one who is feeble among them in that day shall be like David, and the house of David shall be like God, like the angel of the Lord before them. It shall be in that day that I will seek to destroy all the nations that come against Jerusalem. And I will pour on the inhabitants of Jerusalem the Spirit of grace and supplication; then they will look upon Me whom they have pierced; they will mourn for Him as one mourns for his only son, and grieve for Him as one grieves for a firstborn.

In that day a fountain shall be opened for the house of David and for the inhabitants of Jerusalem, for sin and for uncleanness. . . And it shall come to pass in all the land, says the LORD, that two thirds in it shall be cut off and die, But one third shall be left in it: I will bring the one third through the fire, Will refine them as silver is refined, And test them as gold is tested. They will call on My name, and I will answer them. I will say, 'This is My people'; And each one will say, 'The LORD is my God' " (Zechariah 12:8-10; 13:1,8-9 NKJ).

This now completes our brief survey of God's special call of the Jewish people and the Abrahamic covenant to which the whole movement of world history is tied. In the next chapter, we are going to get an overview of how this covenant affects God's plan for Israel.

Chapter 3—God's Covenant With Abraham

Study Guide 2

1. Write out Genesis 12:1-3.

   Get out of your country . . .

2. Describe the type of covenant God made with Abraham.

   Blood. Un binding

3. List and explain the three major promises that God made to Abraham as part of the Abrahamic covenant.

   a. *Land - Isreal*

   b. *Nation - People (12 Tribes- Jacob)*

   c. *blessing - Jesus*

4

God's Plan For Israel

One of the reasons for writing this book is to help you to see the world situation in which we live through the eyes of God rather than the evening news. *God's covenant with Abraham is the key to the door of understanding of world history and the future of planet earth.*

As we've just discovered, this covenant was a binding, literal, unconditional, everlasting covenant. And God is a covenant keeping God. Yet, as we're learning, the promises God made to Abraham have never been completely fulfilled to the degree that God intended.

It is true that God brought the Jews out of Egypt and into their land. But they never fully controlled it as God promised Abraham. They also became a great nation under King Solomon, but they soon became dominated by the Gentile world powers. Jesus did come as their Messiah and establish the new covenant. But the Jews did not accept Him and, therefore, missed their blessing.

In spite of the failure of the Jews to honor the covenant, God must honor His commitment to Abraham. He must keep His promises. He must do whatever is necessary to bring the covenant promises to fulfillment. *As we look into the world through the pages of the Bible, we see that God is absolutely in control of world events and is moving them around the Jew to bring these promises to pass.*

From Abraham To Moses

When God made His covenant with Abraham, He told him that his descendants would be slaves in a strange country, but that He would deliver them with great wealth (Genesis 15:13-14). We learn from the Bible that this strange country was Egypt.

In the previous chapter, we noted that one of Jacob's sons was named Joseph. Joseph's brothers sold him as a slave into Egypt. But after much personal tribulation, Joseph rose to a prominent position in Egypt. Because of a famine, Jacob (Israel) and his family made their way to Egypt where Joseph cared for them.

While in Egypt, the Jews grew from a family of seventy to a nation of several million. This is one of the reasons why God allowed them to stay in Egypt. They had to have time to grow numerically so they would be able to defeat the nations that were in the land which God had promised to them.

Because of their numbers, Pharaoh felt threatened by them and made them slaves, just as God had said would happen to them. As time passed, the Jews began to cry out to God for deliverance. God remembered His covenant with Abraham and chose Moses to lead the Jewish people out of Egyptian bondage (Exodus 2:24-25). This was around the year 1491 BC.

It was only a few weeks journey from Egypt to the promised land. But it took the Jews forty years to make the trip. This was because they failed to trust and obey God. God told them to go in and take the land. But instead of doing so, they sent in twelve spies to scout it out. Ten of the spies reported that the inhabitants of the land were invincible. Only Joshua and Caleb were willing to go in and take the land as God had instructed them to do. But the people didn't listen. As a result, they spent forty years wandering in the desert until that entire generation died, except for Joshua and Caleb.

Renewing The Covenant

The long desert journey had finally come to an end. It was time for the new generation of Jews who were born during the forty years to enter the land. This generation of Jews had not been around when God renewed His covenant with their parents. So it was necessary that God confirm the covenant with them.

Moses called them together for one last time before he died. He reminded them of how God entered into covenant with their father Abraham. *He spoke of blessings if they obeyed God, but warned them of judgement and curses if they disobeyed* (Deuteronomy 28). This took place in about the year 1451 BC.

Moses was going to hand over the leadership to Joshua. But before doing so, he spoke to them about their future. Here is what he said:

"Take heed to yourselves, lest you forget the covenant of the LORD your God, which he made with you, and make a graven image in the form of anything which the LORD your God has forbidden you. For the LORD your God is a devouring fire, a jealous God.

When you beget children and children's children, and have grown old in the land, if you act corruptly by making a graven image in the form of anything, and by doing what is evil in the sight of the LORD your God, so as to provoke him to anger, I call heaven and earth to witness against you this day, that you will soon utterly perish from off the land which you are going over the

Jordan to possess; you will not live long upon it, but will be utterly destroyed. And the LORD will scatter you among the peoples, and you will be left few in number among the nations where the LORD will drive you. And there you will serve gods of wood and stone, the work of men's hands, that neither see, nor hear, nor eat, nor smell. But from there you will seek the LORD your God, and you will find him, if you search after him with all your heart and with all your soul. When you are in tribulation, and all these things come upon you in the latter days, you will return to the LORD your God and obey his voice, for the LORD your God is a merciful God; he will not fail you or destroy you or forget the covenant with your fathers which he swore to them" (Deuteronomy 4:23-31 RSV).

As Moses continued to speak, he added this further prediction concerning the future of the Jews:

"Now it shall come to pass, when all these things come upon you, the blessing and the curse which I have set before you, and you call them to mind among all the nations where the LORD your God drives you,

and you return to the LORD your God and obey His voice, according to all that I command you today, you and your children, with all your heart and with all your soul,

that the LORD your God will bring you back from captivity, and have compassion on you, and gather you again from all the nations where the LORD your God has scattered you.

If any of you are driven out to the farthest parts under heaven, from there the LORD your God will gather you, and from there He will bring you.

Then the LORD your God will bring you to the land which your fathers possessed, and you shall possess it. He will prosper you and multiply you more than your fathers.

And the LORD your God will circumcise your heart and the heart of your descendants, to love the LORD your God with all your heart and with all your soul, that you may live" (Deuteronomy 30:1-6 NKJ).

A Ten-Point Prediction

In this long address, Moses looked far into the future and made a prediction about the destiny of the Jewish people. This prediction was based on God's covenant with Abraham. It included ten statements that accurately describe the past, present and future of the Jews. It was a sweeping declaration of God's plan for Israel.

These ten statements were:

1. *The Jews will break the covenant*
2. *God will drive them from their land*
3. *God will scatter them among the nations*
4. *Jews will be few in number among the nations*
5. *Jews will serve other gods*
6. *God will preserve a remnant of the Jews throughout history for the latter days*
7. *God will bring the Jews back to their land*
8. *The Jews will go through tribulation*
9. *The Jews will return to God*
10. *God will remember His covenant*

What an amazing prediction. Keep in mind that Moses made it before the Jews even got into their land. Yet here Moses is telling them what's going to happen to them afterward. And as we study world history, we see that this is exactly what happened to the Jews. The Bible makes these statements predicting the history of the Jews long before the Jews had a history.

Only God would know their future. So if we can see how the history of the Jews has been just what God said it would be, then surely we can see that their future, and ours as well, will be just as God says in the Bible. The obvious conclusion we must come to is that *God is in charge of history*.

In chapters five through fourteen, we're going to briefly

consider each of these ten statements. We'll do so by examining other Scriptures that give further details concerning their fulfillment, point out how the prediction was actually fulfilled in history, is now being fulfilled, and will be fulfilled in the future. It's an amazing story!

Chapter 4—God's Plan For Israel

Study Guide 3

1. State the Scripture reference where we find Moses giving his great sermon predicting the future of the Jews.

   Deuteronomy 30 1-6

2. List the ten points that Moses included in his sermon.

   a. Jews break covenant

   b. Driven from land

   c. Scatter Jews among nations

   d. Few in number among nations

   e. Serve other Gods

   f. Preserve remnant of Jews through History for latter Days.

   g. God will bring Jews back to land

   h. Jews will go through tribulation

   i. Jews will return to God

   j. God will remember his covenant

5

Jews Will Break The Covenant

The very first statement Moses makes in this ten-point prediction is that the Jews will break the covenant. He says the way they will break the covenant is by *worshiping idols.* You see, the very first commands that God gave the Jews were that they were not to worship idols. Here are God's words:

> "You shall have no other gods before Me. You shall not make for yourself any carved image, or any likeness of anything that is in heaven above, or that is in the earth beneath, or that is in the water under the earth; You shall not bow down to them nor serve them. For I, the LORD your God, am a jealous God. . ." (Exodus 20:3-5 NKJ).

We see the reason God said they were not to worship idols was that He is a jealous God. God is not jealous in the negative sense of the word as man is jealous. *He is jealous in that the covenant required the Jews to give their devotion to God alone.* There was no room for any rivalry. This is the same type of covenant relationship a man and woman make in a marriage. Their commitment is to each other exclusively and there can be no rivals. If one of the marriage partners gives their devotion to another, they have broken the marriage covenant. Idolatry, therefore, is religious adultery and harlotry.

God said to His covenant people:

"For you must worship no other gods, but only Jehovah, for he is a God who claims absolute loyalty and exclusive devotion" (Exodus 34:14 TLB).

Divine Warnings

When God was preparing the Jews to enter the land, He told them to destroy all the idols of the previous inhabitants.

Exodus 23:24 reads:

"You must not worship the gods of these other nations, nor sacrifice to them in any way, and you must not follow the evil example of these people; you must utterly conquer them and break down their shameful idols" (TLB).

God repeated this warning to the people many times before He led them into the land. *Obedience to this instruction was necessary for them to stay there.* (See Leviticus 19:4; 26:1; Numbers 33:52; Deuteronomy 5:7-10; 6:14-15; 7:3-5; 11:16; 30:17; Joshua 23:7; 24:16-27).

An Unfaithful People

After Moses died, Joshua led the people into the promised land. As long as Joshua and the elders who served with him were alive, the people were outwardly faithful to God (Joshua 24:31). But afterwards, they began to worship the heathen gods and live immorally. This shows that, as a nation, *their hearts never really turned toward God.*

We read in the book of Judges:

"They did many things which the Lord had expressly forbidden, including the worshiping of heathen gods. They abandoned Jehovah, the God loved and worshiped by their ancestors——the God who had brought them out of Egypt. Instead, they were worshiping and bowing low before the idols of the neighboring nations. So the anger of the Lord flamed out against all Israel. He left them to the mercy of their enemies, for they had departed from Jehovah and were worshiping Baal and the Ashtaroth idols" (Judges 2:11-14 TLB).

This was the darkest period in the young nation's history. Everyone did what was right in his own eyes (Judges 21:25). God then used the enemies of Israel as a means of disciplining them in order to bring them to repentence. When the people were oppressed, they repented, and God sent judges to deliver them from their enemies. These judges were mostly military leaders. There were thirteen of these deliverers. God ruled Israel through them. But the people would soon forget and go back to their sinful ways. This cycle continued from about the years 1400 to 1101 BC (Judges 2:15-19).

A Call To Repentance

God then raised up a young man named Samuel to guide the Jews during the transition period from the time of the judges to the time of the monarchy. Samuel was a true prophet of God who kept the nation together during this difficult period. The people trusted Samuel. He persuaded them to repent of their idol worship and immorality and turn back to God (1 Samuel 7:3-4). Samuel served God and the nation of Israel from about the years 1100 to 1055 BC.

How did the nation once again turn its back on God and slide into idol worship? It happened like this. When Samuel grew old, he expected his sons to succeed him. But they were wicked, so the people wouldn't follow them. They demanded that Samuel appoint a king to govern them. Although this was not God's desire for the people, He directed Samuel to appoint Saul as the first king of Israel. Saul ruled from about 1096 to 1056 BC. He was proud and disobeyed God. But because of Samuel's influence, Saul did not lead the nation away from God.

During Saul's rule, God chose David as His king to succeed Saul. Samuel anointed David while David was still a young shepherd boy. Although David often failed God, he loved God and sincerely wanted to please Him. The New Testament Scriptures tell us that David was a man after God's own heart (Acts 13:22). David ruled from about 1056 to 1016 BC.

Just before David died, he appointed his son Solomon to succeed him as king. Solomon was very wise and led Israel into her greatest period of glory. His outstanding achievement was building the temple in Israel.

Solomon's Folly

But Solomon also brought disaster on the nation. Contrary to God's instruction (Deuteronomy 7:3-5), *Solomon took many foreign wives who led him and the nation into idol worship from which they never recovered* (1 Kings 11:1-13). In order to support his many wives and finance their idol worship, Solomon oppressed the people with excessive taxes and forced labor. They finally revolted in 976 BC at Solomon's death, and the kingdom was divided into north and south (1 Kings 12).

The northern kingdom was called Israel. It consisted of ten tribes with Samaria as its capital. It had nineteen kings who were of nine different families. All of these kings were evil and led the people into idol worship.

The southern kingdom was called Judah. It consisted of the two tribes of Judah and Benjamin, with Jerusalem as its capital. It had nineteen kings and one queen—all from the line of David. Although Judah honored the covenant more so than their brothers to the north, they too eventually turned away from God. This forced God to bring judgement on them as well.

Scripture References

We are deeply saddened and heartbroken to see how the Jews broke their covenant with God. God raised up many prophets to warn them. And although there was always a godly remnant, the nation as a whole did not heed their words. Here are a few Scriptures describing the nation's idolatry. I list them with great sorrow and meekness knowing that we Gentiles have not done any better.

Isaiah wrote:

"You worship your idols with great zeal beneath the shade of every tree, and slay your children as human sacrifices down in the valleys, under overhanging rocks. Your gods are the smooth stones in the valleys. You worship them and they, not I, are your inheritance. Does all this make me happy? You have committed adultery on the tops of the mountains, for you worship idols there, deserting me. Behind closed doors you set your idols up and worship someone other than me. This is adultery, for you are giving these idols your love, instead of loving me" (Isaiah 57:5-8 TLB).

(See also Isaiah 27:7-9; 44:9-20.)

Jeremiah said:

"I have sent you prophet after prophet to tell you to turn back from your wicked ways and to stop worshiping other gods and that if you obeyed, then I would let you live in peace here in the land I gave to you and your fathers. But you wouldn't listen or obey" (Jeremiah 35:15 TLB).

(See also Jeremiah 2:10-11, 20, 26-28; 3:8-9, 20; 7:3-11, 29-31; 11:9-17; 32:32-25.)

Ezekiel warned:

"Son of dust, these men worship idols in their

47

hearts——should I let them ask me anything? Tell them, the Lord God says: I the Lord will personally deal with anyone in Israel who worships idols and then comes to ask my help. For I will punish the minds and hearts of those who turn from me to idols.

Therefore warn them that the Lord God says: Repent and destroy your idols, and stop worshiping them in your hearts. I the Lord will personally punish everyone, whether the people of Israel or the foreigners living among you, who reject me for idols, and then comes to a prophet to ask for my help and advice. I will turn upon him and make a terrible example of him, destroying him; and you shall know that I am the Lord" (Ezekiel 14:3-8 TLB).

(See also Ezekiel 8:6-18; 16; 20:27-31; 23:30, 36-39.) Hosea spoke:

"And now the people disobey more and more. They melt their silver to mold into idols, formed with skill by the hands of men. 'Sacrifice to these!' they say—— men kissing calves! They shall disappear like morning mist, like dew that quickly dries away, like chaff blown by the wind, like a cloud of smoke" (Hosea 13:2-3 TLB).

(See also Hosea 4:11-19; 8:2-5; 10:1-3.)

Chapter 5 - Jews Will Break The Covenant

Study Guide 4

1. State what major sin God warned the Jews against.

   Breaking the covenant

2. State what sin the Jews committed that caused them to break the covenant.

   Worshiping Idols

3. State how Solomon brought disaster on the Jewish nation.

   Married foreign wives + taxed the people.

6

God Will Drive Them From Their Land

Because of their idol worship, Moses declared that God would drive the Hebrews from their land. As we've already mentioned, God's covenant is unconditional. However, the benefits or blessings of the covenant are conditional based on obedience. Any one generation of Jews could break the covenant by worshiping idols. That generation would miss the blessings of the covenant. But their disobedience could not annul the covenant itself. It would still be in force for the next generation of Jews, if they chose to honor it.

But if succeeding generations did not honor the covenant, God would (1) drive them from their land (2) take away their sovereignty as a nation (3) allow their sins to blind their eyes and deafen their ears spiritually speaking so that they would not recognize their Messiah. They would miss the blessings of the new covenant which the Messiah would offer. Unfortunately, this is exactly what happened.

Both Isaiah and Jesus spoke of this problem. Isaiah said:

"Also I heard the voice of the Lord saying: 'Whom shall I send, And who will go for Us?' Then I said, 'Here am I! Send me.'

And He said, 'Go, and tell this people: Keep on hearing, but do not understand; Keep on seeing, but do not perceive.

Make the heart of this people dull, And their ears heavy, And shut their eyes; Lest they see with their eyes, And hear with their ears, And understand with their heart, And return and be healed" (Isaiah 6:8-10 NKJ).

"Therefore the LORD said: 'Inasmuch as these people draw near to Me with their mouths, And honor Me with their lips, But have removed their hearts far from Me, and their fear toward Me is taught by the commandment of men,

Therefore, behold, I will again do a marvelous work Among this people, A marvelous work and a wonder; For the wisdom of their wise men shall perish, And the understanding of their prudent men shall be hidden' " (Isaiah 29:13-14 NKJ).

Jesus referred to Isaiah's words in the following New Testament Scriptures:

"And the disciples came and said to Him, 'Why do You speak to them in parables?'

He answered and said to them, 'Because it has been give to you to know the mysteries of the kingdom of heaven, but to them it has not been given.

For whoever has, to him more will be given, and he will have abundance; but whoever does not have, even what he has will be taken away from him.

Therefore I speak to them in parables, because seeing

they do not see, and hearing they do not hear, nor do they understand.

And in them the prophecy of Isaiah is fulfilled, which says: 'Hearing you will hear and shall not understand, And seeing you will see and not perceive;

For the heart of this people has grown dull. Their ears are hard of hearing, And their eyes they have closed, Lest they should see with their eyes and hear with their ears, Lest they should understand with their heart and turn, So that I should heal them' " (Matthew 13:10-15 NKJ).

"Hypocrites! Well did Isaiah prophesy about you, saying: 'These people draw near to Me with their mouth, And honor Me with their lips, But their heart is far from Me. And in vain they worship Me, Teaching as doctrines the commandments of men' " (Matthew 15:7-9 NKJ).

Because of their disobedience, God raised up Gentile nations and used them as His means of chastening the Jews. This has always been one of God's ways of dealing with the Jews, as it still is today. Let's see how God did this as recorded in the Hebrew Scriptures.

The Assyrian Whip

The prophet Isaiah tells of God's plan to use the Assyrians to conquer the northern kingdom (Israel) and drive the people from the land. Isaiah writes on behalf of God:

"Assyria is the whip of my anger; his military strength is my weapon upon this godless nation, doomed and damned; he will enslave them and plunder them and trample them like dirt beneath his feet. But the king of Assyria will not know it is I who sent him. He will merely think he is attacking my people as part of his plan to conquer the world." (Isaiah 10:5-7 TLB).

The book of 2 Kings records the fulfillment of this chastisement by God which took place in 721 BC. We find the following account given in the Living Bible:

"Now the land of Israel was filled with Assyrian troops for three years besieging Samaria, the capital city of Israel. Finally, in the ninth year of King Hoshea's reign, Samaria fell and the people of Israel were exiled to Assyria. They were placed in colonies in the city of Halah and along the banks of the Habor River in Gozan, and among the cities of the Medes.

This disaster came upon the nation of Israel because the people worshiped other gods, thus sinning against the Lord their God who had brought them safely out of their slavery in Egypt. They had followed the evil customs of the nations which the Lord had cast out before them. The people of Israel had also secretly done many things that were wrong, and they had built altars to other gods throughout the land. They had placed obelisks and idols at the top of every hill and under every green tree; and they had burned incense to the gods of the very nations which the Lord had cleared out of the land when Israel came in. So the people of Israel had done many evil things, and the Lord was very angry. Yes, they worshiped idols, despite the Lord's specific and repeated warnings.

Again and again the Lord had sent prophets to warn both Israel and Judah to turn from their evil ways; he had warned them to obey his commandments which he had given them to their ancestors through these prophets, but Israel wouldn't listen. The people were as stubborn as their ancestors and refused to believe in the Lord their God. They rejected his laws and the covenant he had made with their ancestors, and despised all his warnings. They defied all the commandments of the Lord their God and made two calves from molten gold. They made detestable, shameful idols and worshiped Baal and the sun, moon, and stars. They even burned their own sons and daughters to death on the altars of Molech; they consulted fortune-tellers and used magic and sold themselves to evil. So the Lord was very angry. He swept them from his sight until only the tribe of Judah remained in the land.

But even Judah refused to obey the commandments of the Lord their God; they too walked in the same evil paths as Israel had. So the Lord rejected all the descendants of Jacob. He punished them by delivering them to their attackers until they were destroyed. For Israel split off from the kingdom of David and chose Jeroboam I (the son of Nebat) as its king. Then Jeroboam drew Israel away from following the Lord. He made them sin a great sin, and the people of Israel never quit doing the evil things that Jeroboam led them into, until the Lord finally swept them away, just as all his prophets had warned would happen. So Israel was carried off to the land of Assyria where they remain to this day" (2 Kings 17:5-23 TLB).

The Babylonian Conquest

The prophet Jeremiah had the sad task of predicting the downfall of the southern kingdom. God used Babylon to drive them from the land. Jeremiah writes:

"Again and again down through the years, God has sent you his prophets, but you have refused to hear. Each time the message was this: Turn from the evil road you are traveling and from the evil things you are doing. Only then can you continue to live here in this land which the Lord gave to you and to your ancestors forever. Don't anger me by worshiping idols; but if you are true to me, then I'll not harm you. But you won't listen; you have gone ahead and made me furious with your idols. So you have brought upon yourselves all the evil that has come your way.

And now the Lord God of Hosts says, 'Because you have not listened to me, I will gather together all the armies of the north under Nebuchadnezzar, king of

Babylon (I have appointed him as my deputy), and I will bring them all against this land and its people and against the other nations near you and make you a byword of contempt forever. I will take away your joy, your gladness and your wedding feasts; your businesses shall fail and all your homes shall lie in silent darkness. This entire land shall become a desolate wasteland; all the world will be shocked at the disaster that befalls you. Israel and her neighboring lands shall serve the king of Babylon for seventy years' " (Jeremiah 25:4-11 TLB).

We find the fulfillment of this divine chastisement recorded in the book of Chronicles. The Babylon siege began in 606 BC and was completed in 586 BC. We read in 2 Chronicles:

"All the important people of the nation, including the High Priests, worshiped the heathen idols of the surrounding nations, thus polluting the Temple of the Lord in Jerusalem. Jehovah the God of their fathers sent his prophets again and again to warn them, for he had compassion on his people and on his Temple. But the people mocked these messengers of God and despised their words, scoffing at the prophets until the anger of the Lord could no longer be restrained, and there was no longer any remedy.

"Then the Lord brought the king of Babylon against them and killed their young men, even going after them right into the Temple, and had no pity upon them, killing even young girls and old men. The Lord used the king of Babylon to destroy them completely. He also took home with him all the items, great and small, used in the Temple, and treasures from both the Temple and the palace, and took with him all the royal princes. Then his army burned the Temple and broke down the walls of Jerusalem and burned all the palaces and destroyed all the valuable Temple utensils. Those who survived were taken away to Babylon as slaves to the king and his sons until the kingdom of Persia conquered Babylon" (2 Chronicles 36:14-20 TLB).

Scripture References

Time after time God called His covenant people to turn from their sins. He sent prophet after prophet to warn them. But they refused to repent. Instead, they drifted further and further from God until they became just as evil as the original inhabitants of the land.

God in His goodness was merciful and longsuffering with them. But there came a point in the Jews' rebellion, when God knew they would never repent (Hosea 7:13-16). He had no other choice but to carry out the warnings which He had given them. Some of these warnings are listed below:

"I will revenge the breaking of my covenant by bringing war against you. You will flee to your cities, and I will send a plague among you there; and you will be conquered by your enemies . . . and I will destroy the altars on the hills where you worship your idols, and I will cut down your incense altars, leaving your dead bodies to rot among your idols; and I will abhor you. I will make your cities desolate, and destroy your places of worship, and will not respond to your incense offerings. Yes, I will desolate your land; your enemies shall live in it, utterly amazed at what I have done to you" (Leviticus 26;25,30-32 TLB).

"But beware that your hearts do not turn from God to worship other gods. For if you do, the anger of the Lord will be hot against you, and he will shut the heavens——there will be no rain and no harvest, and you will quickly perish from the good land the Lord has given you. . .

The Lord will cause you to be defeated by your enemies. You will march out to battle gloriously, but flee before your enemies in utter confusion; and you will be tossed to and fro among all the nations of the earth" (Deuteronomy 11:16-17;28:25 TLB).

"But later on, the Lord will bring a terrible curse on you and on your nation and your family. There will be terror, such as had not been known since the division of Solomon's empire into Israel and Judah——the might king of Assyria will come with his great army! At that time the Lord will whistle for the army of Upper Egypt, and of Assyria too, to swarm down upon you like flies and destroy you, like bees to sting and to kill. They will come in vast hordes, spreading across the whole land, even into the desolate valleys and caves and thorny parts, as well as to all your fertile acres. In that day the Lord will take this "razor"—these Assyrians you have hired to save you—and use it on you to shave off everything you have: your land, your crops, your people" (Isaiah 7:17-20 TLB).

"I am calling the armies of the kingdoms of the north to come to Jerusalem and set their thrones at the gates of the city and all along its walls, and in all the other cities of Judah. This is the way I will punish my people for deserting me and for worshiping other Gods—yes, idols they themselves have made" (Jeremiah 1:15-16 TLB).

"See I will bring a distant nation against you, O Israel, says the Lord—a mighty nation, an ancient nation whose language you don't understand. Their weapons are deadly; the men are all mighty. And they shall eat your harvest and your children's bread, and your flocks of sheep and herds of cattle, yes, and your grapes and figs; and they shall sack your walled cities that you think are safe.

But I will not completely blot you out. So says the Lord. And when your people ask, 'Why is it that the Lord is doing this to us?' then you shall say, 'You rejected him and gave yourself to other gods while in your land; now you must be slaves to foreigners in their lands' " (Jeremiah 5:15-19 TLB).

"And when you tell the people all these things and they ask, 'Why has the Lord decreed such terrible things against us? What have we done to merit such treatment? What is our sin against the Lord our God?' tell them the Lord's reply is this: 'Because your fathers forsook me. They worshiped other gods and served them; they did not keep my laws, and you have been worse than your fathers were! You follow evil to your heart's content and refuse to listen to me. Therefore I will throw you out of this land and chase you into a foreign land where neither you nor your fathers have been before, and there you can go ahead and worship your idols all you like—and I will grant you no favors" (Jeremiah 16:10-13 TLB)!

"The Lord God says, 'This illustrates what will happen to Jerusalem, for she has turned away from my laws and has been even more wicked then the nations surrounding her.' Therefore the Lord God says, I, even I, am against you and will punish you publicly while all the nations watch. Because of the terrible sins you have committed, I will punish you more terribly than I have ever done before or will ever do again. Fathers will eat their own sons, and sons will eat their fathers; and those who survive will be scattered into all the world.

For I promise you: Because you have defiled my Temple with your idols and evil sacrifices, therefore I will not spare you nor pity you at all. One-third of you will die from famine and disease; one-third will be slaughtered by the enemy; and one-third I will scatter to the winds, sending the sword of the enemy chasing after you. Then at last my anger will be appeased. And all Israel will know that what I threaten, I do.

So I will make a public example of you before all the surrounding nations and before everyone traveling past the ruins of the land. You will become a laughing-stock to the world and an awesome example to everyone, for all to see what happens when the Lord turns against an entire nation in furious rebuke. I, the Lord, have spoken it" (Ezekiel 5:5-15 TLB).

"Therefore the Lord God says: You think this city is an iron shield? No, it isn't! It will not protect you. Your slain will lie within it, but you will be dragged out and slaughtered. I will expose you to the war you have so greatly feared, says the Lord God, and I will take you from Jerusalem and hand you over to foreigners who will carry out my judgements against you. You will be slaughtered all the way to the borders of Israel, and you will know I am the Lord. No, this city will not be an iron shield for you, and you safe within. I will chase you even to the borders of Israel, and you will know I am the Lord—you who have not obeyed me, but rather have copied the nations all around you" (Ezekiel 11:7-12 TLB).

Chapter 6—God Will Drive Them From Their Land

Study Guide 5

1. Name the Gentile power that God used to conquer the northern kingdom (Israel).

   Syria

2. Name the Gentile power that God used to conquer the southern kingdom (Judah).

   Babylon

3. State why the Jewish leaders did not recognize Jesus as the Messiah.

   God allowed their sins to blind their eyes and deafen their ears. (Spiritually speaking.)

7

God Will Scatter Them Among The Nations

God used Assyria and Babylon to drive the Jews from their land and to begin their scattering among the nations. The Abrahamic covenant, though still in force, had come to a standstill.

God had decreed that the Jews would be captive in Babylon for seventy years (2 Chronicles 36:21; Jeremiah 25:12; 29:10). At the end of the seventy year period, God raised up the Persian Empire for the purpose of freeing the Jews from their captivity and allowing them to return to their homeland. The Persians, under King Cyrus, soundly defeated the Babylonians in 536 BC. God then put the desire in King Cyrus' heart to allow the Jews to return home (2 Chronicles 36:22-23).

Comfort In Babylon

There were three Jewish expeditions from Babylon back to the land of Israel. The first of these was led by Zerubbabel in the year 536 BC. But only about 50,000 Jews accompanied him (Ezra 2:64-65). Ezra led the second return in 458 BC, but only 1,750 men plus women and children accompanied him (Ezra 8). The last expedition was led by Nehemiah in the year 445 BC (Nehemiah 2:1-8). Although some exiles from the northern kingdom also returned during this time, apparently there was no organized return from Assyria.

So we see that not many wanted to return home. *They had become comfortable in Babylon.* Returning home to rebuild the nation was just too much of a challenge for most of the Jews. This is much like the attitude many Jewish people have today. Some have returned to the land, but most have chosen to remain among the Gentiles.

Jews and Greeks

When God was through using Cyrus, He raised up Alexander the Great and established Greece as the next Gentile power. The Jews fared well under the Greeks. As they entered into the mainstream of Greek life, they were free to travel throughout the Greek Empire.

Alexander ruled from 333-323 BC. When he died, his kingdom was divided among his generals who constantly warred against each other for territorial control. Unfortunately, the land of Israel was geographically located between the warring factions. The Jewish remnant who had returned to the land were caught in the middle. This lasted until the year 63 BC when the Roman general Pompey established Roman rule over the Jews in Israel and worldwide rule in 30 BC.

The Great Scattering

Although the Assyrians and Babylonians drove the Jews from the land, *it was left to the Romans to totally and completely scatter them among the nations.* This great scattering, or dispersion, began in 70 AD. when the Roman military, under the leadership of Titus, responded to an internal revolt by the Jews. The Romans were merciless in their siege, slaughtering over one million Jews, devasting the city and leveling the temple. Most of the survivors were sold as slaves to foreign merchants who carried them off to the various nations of the world.

You would think this would have completely destroyed the Jewish will to resist. But it didn't. A new hope for freedom arose a generation later. This hope was in the form of a would-be military Messiah by the name of Simon bar Kochba. Simon bar Kochba claimed to be that greater Son of David who would overthrow the Roman yoke of bondage and once again establish the throne of David in Jerusalem. He was aided in his quest by the honored Rabbi Akiba who convinced the struggling zealots to follow bar Kochba. This again brought the wrath of the Romans against the Jews. And again, the Romans, under Emperor Hadrian, butchered them unmercifully, finishing the slaughter in 135 AD.

The famine in Israel was so bad that the Jews ate the flesh of their own family members just as God said they would (Leviticus 26:29; Deuteronomy 28:53-57; Jeremiah 19:9; Ezekiel 5:10). The glut of Jews on the slave market was so great that many of them were not even bought, as God predicted in Deuteronomy 28:68.

The strongest Jews who survived were sold as slaves to the same foreign merchants who carried off their parents. *Jerusalem was declared off-limits to the Jews who were now forbidden to live in the land God promised them.* Thus was fulfilled God's word by the prophets, "I will scatter you among the nations." As a further insult to the Jews, Hadrian renamed the land of Israel after their ancient enemy the Philistines. He called it—*Palestine.*

Scripture References

Some Scriptures that predicted this scattering are as follows:

"I will scatter you out among the nations, destroying

65

you with war as you go. Your land shall be desolate and your cities destroyed.

And for those who are left alive, I will cause them to be dragged away to distant lands as prisoners of war, and slaves. There they will live in constant fear. The sound of a leaf driven in the wind will send them fleeing as though chased by a man with a sword; they shall fall when no one is pursuing them. Yes, though none pursue they shall stumble over each other in flight, as though fleeing in battle, with no power to stand before their enemies. You shall perish among the nations and be destroyed among your enemies. Those left shall pine away in enemy lands because of their sins, the same sins as those of their fathers" (Leviticus 26:33, 36-39 TLB).

"The Lord will cause you to be defeated by your enemies. You shall march out to battle gloriously, but flee before your enemies in utter confusion; and you will be tossed to and fro among all the nations of the earth.

"For the Lord will scatter you among all the nations from one end of the earth to the other. There you will worship heathen gods that neither you nor your ancestors have known, gods made of wood and stone! There among those nations you shall find no rest, but the Lord will give you trembling hearts, darkness, and bodies wasted from sorrow and fear. Your lives will hang in doubt. You will live night and day in fear, and will have no reason to believe that you will see the morning light. In the morning you will say, 'O that night were here!' And in the evening you will say, 'O that morning were here!' You will say this because of the awesome horrors surrounding you" (Deuteronomy 28:25,64-67 TLB).

"Therefore I will send you into exile far away because you neither know nor care that I have done so much for you. Your great and honored men will starve, and the common people will die of thirst" (Isaiah 5:13 TLB).

"Then I said, 'Lord, how long will it be before they are ready to listen?' And he replied, 'Not until their cities are destroyed—without a person left—and the whole country is an utter wasteland, and they are all taken away as slaves to other countries far away, and all the land of Israel lies deserted" (Isaiah 6:11-12 TLB).

"Why is the land a wilderness so that no one dares even to travel through?

'Because,' the Lord replies, 'my people have forsaken my commandments and not obeyed my laws. Instead they have done what ever they pleased and worshiped the idols of Baal, as their fathers told them to. Therefore this is what the Lord of Hosts, the God of Israel, says: Lo, I will feed them with bitterness and give them poison to drink. I will scatter them around the world, to be strangers in distant lands; and even there the sword of destruction shall chase them until I have utterly destroyed them' " (Jeremiah 9:13-16 TLB).

"MY PEOPLE sin as though commanded to, as though their evil were laws chiseled with an iron pen or diamond point upon their stony hearts or on corners of their altars. Their youths do not forget to sin, worshiping idols beneath each tree, high in the mountains or in the open country down below. And so I will give all your treasuries to your enemies as the price that you must pay for all your sins. And the wonderful heritage I reserved for you will slip out of your hand, and I will send you away as slaves to your enemies in distant lands. For you have kindled a fire of my anger that shall burn forever" (Jeremiah 17:1-4 TLB).

"And I will scatter them around the world. And in every nation where I have placed them they will be cursed and hissed and mocked, for they refuse to listen to me though I spoke to them again and again through my prophets" (Jeremiah 29:18-19 TLB).

"But I will let a few of my people escape—to be scattered among the nations of the world" (Ezekiel 6:8 TLB).

"And I exiled them to many lands; that is how I punished them for the evil way they lived" (Ezekiel 36:19 TLB).

"My God will destroy the people of Israel because they will not listen or obey. They will be wandering Jews, homeless among the nations" (Hosea 9:17 TLB).

"The Lord's reply is this:. . .You yourself will die in a heathen land, and the people of Israel will certainly become slaves in exile, far from their land" (Amos 7:17 TLB).

Chapter 7—God Will Scatter Them Among The Nations

Study Guide 6

1. Explain how the Jews responded to the decree by Cyrus that allowed them to return to their land.

   They became comfortable in Babylon and did not want to come back and rebuild

2. State what Jewish life was like under Alexander's rule.

   Jews were free to travel throughout Greece

3. Explain what happened in 70 and 135 AD.

   Dispersion by Romans, (70 AD)
   Slaughter by Romans in (135 AD)

8

Jews Few In Number Among The Nations

We noted in an earlier chapter that Abraham is the father of both the Jews and the Arabs. He is the father of the Arabs through Ishmael and the Jews through Isaac. Abraham fathered these two sons around the year 2,000 BC. This means that both the Arabs and the Jews have been in existence for about 6,000 years.

Any people who have been around that long should number as the sand in the sea and the stars in the sky just as God had promised Abraham they would. This is true for the Arabs. The present population of the Arab world is approximately 150 million. You would expect the same for the Jews. But it's not. The total Jewish population in the world as of 1982 is only about fifteen million.

Why is this so? Why so many more Arabs than Jews? It

can only be because of God's judgement upon the Jews for dishonoring the covenant. *From 70 and 135 AD to 1948 when Israel became a nation, the Jews have lived in exile from their land, few in number at the mercy of God and their Gentile masters.*

Of the approximate fifteen million Jews who are alive today, about six million live in the United States, three million live in Russia, three million in Israel and the remaining are still scattered throughout the nations.

Times Of The Gentiles

Jesus spoke of this period of Gentile domination of the Jews as the *"Times of the Gentiles."* Jesus was asked by His followers when He would establish the kingdom of God and David on planet earth. He responded by saying that the Gentile nations would first have their moment of glory. But their dominance of world affairs would be characterized by unrighteousness. When this unrighteousness had its full course, Jesus said He would return to earth and establish the righteous rule of God. The kingdom of God would then be administered through Israel as the head nation of the earth. This would end the times of the Gentiles.

We read these words from Jesus, "And they will fall by the edge of the sword, and be led away captive into all nations. And Jerusalem will be trampled by the Gentiles until the times of the Gentiles are fulfilled" (Luke 21:24 NKJ).

The times of the Gentiles represents that period in world history when the Gentile nations of the world would rule over Jerusalem and dominate the Jewish people. God would allow this to take place as part of His sovereignty over the flow of history in working out His divine plans and purposes. When one of these nations or empires had served its purpose, God would destroy it because of its evil and raise up another in its place. This cycle would continue throughout the course of world history until God determined to bring it to a close with the second coming of Messiah Jesus.

In the list below, I have identified the major periods of

72

national sovereignty over the city of Jerusalem. These periods involve Gentile domination from the time of Babylon to the second coming of Messiah Jesus. Taken as a whole, they represent the entire period of world history referred to by Jesus as the times of the Gentiles. The only exception to Gentile domination shown on the list is the current control Israel has over Jerusalem. Because Israel is now in control of Jerusalem, we know that the times of the Gentiles are at an end. However, a future Gentile leader called the Antichrist will temporarily take control away from Israel and occupy the city for a brief time. Then Messiah Jesus will come and put an end to Gentile rule.

Times Of The Gentiles

Babylon 606-536 BC
Persia 536-333 BC
Greece 333-63 BC
Rome 63-312 AD
Byzantine 312-637
Moslem 637-1099
Crusades 1099-1291
Mamelukes 1291-1517
Ottoman Turks 1517-1917
British Mandate 1917-1948
Jordan 1948-1967
Israel 1967-?
Antichrist ?
Messiah Jesus ? (1000 years)

The times of the Gentiles are coming to a close as God is preparing to give the nation of Israel her place of worldwide pre-eminence. This is why all the great Gentile nations are having so much difficulty. *I believe in the very near future there will be a worldwide economic, political, social, moral and military collapse of all the Gentile powers.* This will leave a power vacuum that will be filled by Israel's arch enemy—the Antichrist. As we'll discuss in a later chapter, the Antichrist will kill millions of Jews leaving only a few

73

million left alive in fulfillment of Moses' prophecy, "You will be few in number."

Scripture References

The following Scriptures are only a few of many that predicted the Jews would be left few in number throughout history:

"Jehovah will scatter you among the nations, and you will be but few in number" (Deuteronomy 4:27 TLB).

"There will be few of you left, though before you were as numerous as stars. All this if you do not listen to the Lord your God" (Deuteronomy 28:62 TLB).

"If the Lord of Hosts had not stepped in to save a few of us, we would have been wiped out as Sodom and Gomorrah were" (Isaiah 1:9 TLB).

"But Israel be now as many as the sands along the shore, yet only a few of them will be left to return at that time; God has rightly decided to destroy his people. Yes, it has already been decided by the Lord God of Hosts to consume them" (Isaiah 10:22-23 TLB).

"LOOK! THE Lord is overturning the land of Judah and making it a vast wasteland of destruction. See how he is emptying out all its people and scattering them over the face of the earth. Priests and people, servants and masters, slave girls and mistresses, buyers and sellers, lenders and borrowers, bankers and debtors—none will be spared. The land will be completely emptied and looted. The Lord has spoken. The land suffers from the sins of its people. The earth languishes, the crops wither, the skies refuse their rain. The land is defiled by crime; the people have twisted the laws of God and broken his everlasting commands. Therefore the curse of God is upon them; they are left desolate, destroyed by the drought. Few will be left alive" (Isaiah 24:1-6 TLB).

"But I will let a few of my people escape—to be scattered among the nations of the world" (Ezekiel 6:8 TLB).

"And when I scatter them among the nations, then they shall know I am the Lord. But I will spare a few of them from death by war and famine and disease. I will save them to confess to the nations how wicked they have been, and they shall know I am the Lord" (Ezekiel 12:15-16 TLB).

"I will count you carefully and let only a small quota return. And the others—the rebels and all those who sin against me—I will purge from among you. They shall not enter Israel, but I will bring them out of the countries where they are in exile. And when that happens, you will know I am the Lord" (Ezekiel 20:37-38 TLB).

Chapter 8—Jews Few In Number Among The Nations

Study Guide 7

1. State the current approximate worldwide population of Jews.

   15 million

2. List the three major population centers of Jewish people.

   a. *USA*

   b. *Israel*

   c. *Russia*

3. Explain what Jesus meant by the term "Times of the Gentiles."

   The time when the Gentiles will have their "moment in glory" over Jerusalem.

9

Jews Will Serve Other Gods

While the Jews were in Egypt, they were tempted to serve the Egyptian gods. So when God delivered them, He brought plagues against the gods of Egypt to show both the Egyptians and His own people that He alone was God. But a considerable number of the Jews never put away their Egyptian idols (Ezekiel 20:7-8). And you know what happened as a result? It wasn't long after they had left Egypt that they made a golden calf as a physical object of worship. You see, their hearts were still with their idols (Ezekiel 20:16). This angered God so that He was going to destroy them. But Moses interceded on their behalf, and God spared them (Exodus 32).

For the most part, however, they never did really repent. They desired to go back to Egypt. They longed for the idols which their fathers worshiped (Ezekiel 20:24; Amos 5:26-27; Acts 7:39-43).

Even though they sacrificed to God, their hearts were set on their idols. And as we've been painfully learning, they continued their idol worship even after they got into their land. *In fact, except for a brief period under Samuel and David, and other brief revivals, the people worshiped idols almost the entire time they were in the land.* This, of course, is why God exiled them.

Flirting With Idols

But their exile did not put an end to the Jews' love affair with the gods of their pagan neighbors. As we've just noted, only a small number of Jews took advantage of Cyrus' decree allowing them to return to the land. The rest stayed behind in Babylon. *The reason they stayed behind is because they loved Babylon more than they loved God.* If they had loved God, they would have returned to the land.

But even of those who returned, all did not love God. When Ezra led his small group back to Israel, he found that many of those who had earlier accompanied Zerubbabel had married pagan women and were once again polluting themselves with idol worship (Ezra 9; Nehemiah 13). It was only the godly leadership of Ezra and Nehemiah, along with the prophetic voices of Haggai, Zechariah, and Malachi, that turned the people from their sin. Then they renewed the covenant with God promising to serve and obey Him while accepting the consequences if they did not (Nehemiah 9-10).

New Kinds Of Gods

When Alexander the Great crushed the Persian armies in 333 BC, the Jews came under Greek rule. *Through divine providence, Alexander showed favor to the Jews, allowing them to enter into the mainstream of Greek life.* This was both good and bad. It was good in that it gave the Jews considerable freedom to practice their religion while at the same time prosper and multiply. It was bad in that the Greek world-system made major inroads into Jewish life.

Alexander's dream for world conquest went beyond the sphere of the military. He desired to spread Greek philosophy and the culture which it bore to all the world. Alexander wanted his subjects to think Greek, talk Greek and act Greek. Greek philosophy was pagan. It promoted the worship of the twin gods of knowledge and pleasure.

These Greek gods became the new idols of many of the Jews. Greek philosophy and culture first infected the Jews' language, manners, and customs. The Jews begin to speak the Greek language, take Greek names and practice Greek ways. *It wasn't long that Jewish attitudes, morals and religion also became greatly influenced. Many of the Jews began to put away their physical idols and to worship at the shrine of knowledge and pleasure.*

When Rome conquered Greece, their victories were of a military and political nature. But the Greek world view was adopted by the Romans and continued to be the dominant influence over the minds of men. Rome ruled their bodies, but Greece ruled their minds.

When the Romans scattered the Jews into the nations of the world, the Jews took their Greek-influenced religion with them. So that today, even though there has always been a godly remnant of Jews, many are either agnostic or athiest.

Perhaps this is why there are twice as many Jews today in the United States as there are in Israel. Could this be why some number of Russian Jews emigrate to places other than Israel? Perhaps they don't yet have a heart for the land. Possibly they don't have a heart for the land because they may not have a heart for God. And as it was in the days of Ezra, many who have returned to the land today have done so for political reasons, not religious ones. This will change, as we shall soon learn.

79

Scripture References

Some Scriptures that speak of this continued apostasy of the Jews are listed below:

"Jehovah will scatter you among the nations, and you will be but few in number. There, far away, you will worship idols made from wood and stone, idols that neither see nor hear nor eat nor smell" (Deuteronomy 4:27-28 TLB).

"For the Lord will scatter you among all the nations from one end of the earth to the other. There you will worship heathen gods that neither you nor your ancestors have known, gods made of wood and stone" (Deuteronomy 28:64 TLB)!

"Therefore I will throw you out of this land and chase you into a foreign land where neither you nor your fathers have been before, and there you can go ahead and worship your idols all you like—and I will grant you no favors" (Jeremiah 16:13 TLB)!

"What you have in mind will not be done—to be like the nations all around you, serving gods of wood and stone" (Ezekiel 20:32 TLB).

"O Jerusalem, Jerusalem, the city that kills the prophets, and stones all those God sends to her! How often I wanted to gather your children together as a hen gathers her chicks beneath her wings, but you wouldn't let me. And now your house is left to you, desolate. For I tell you this, you will never see me again until you are ready to welcome the one sent to you from God" (Matthew 23:37-39 TLB).

"For you are the children of your father the devil and you love to do the evil things he does. He was a murderer from the beginning and a hater of truth—there is not an iota of truth in him. When he lies, it is perfectly normal; for he is the father of liars. And so when I tell the truth, you just naturally don't believe it" (John 8:44 TLB).

"You stiff-necked heathen! Must you forever resist the Holy Spirit? But your fathers did, and so do you! Name one prophet your ancestors didn't persecute! They even killed the ones who predicted the coming of the Righteous One—the Messiah whom you betrayed and murdered. Yes, and you deliberately destroyed God's laws. . ." (Acts 7:51-53 TLB).

"I know the slander of those opposing you, who say that they are Jews—the children of God—but they aren't for they support the cause of Satan" (Revelation 2:9 TLB).

Chapter 9—Jews Will Serve Other Gods

Study Guide 8

1. State why most of the Jews stayed behind in Babylon rather than returning to their land.

   They enjoyed their life. They were not faithful to God. They loved babylon more than God

2. Explain what the Jews who returned to Babylon did that caused God to be angry with them.

   Married Pagan women & worshiped Pagan Gods.

3. Describe what happened to the Jews when they came under the rule of Alexander the Great.

   They learned Greek way of life as well as the language and the philosophy of the twin Gods of knowledge & pleasure.

10

God Will Preserve A Remnant

In one of her more philosophical moments, Queen Victoria asked her Jewish prime minister the following question, "Can you give me just one verse in the Bible to prove that it's true?" He replied, "Your majesty, I can give you one word—the *Jew!*" He went on to explain how the history of the Jewish people is overwhelming proof that the Bible is the Word of God. There is simply no other explanation for the existence of the Jews today.

That is what this chapter is all about. We are seeing that the prophets of the Bible accurately predicted the history of the Jews long before they even had a history. Part of that prediction was that God would always preserve a remnant of the Jews from one generation to the next. And indeed He has.

As we study the pages of history, we learn that no other ethnic people have ever survived a long-term period of exile from their own country. They were either killed off by their conquerors or assimilated into the culture, with the loss of their identity, never to be heard from again. The Jews are the one exception. *Every Jew alive today is a living testimony and witness to the truth of the Scriptures and the faithfulness of God to keep His covenant.*

Ancient Foes

As we've learned, the Assyrians and Babylonians were used by God to bring about the Jews' first exile. Their armies crushed the Jews, but many survived and were taken captive. Yet even though Cyrus allowed them to return to their land, most remained behind scattered throughout the Persian Empire.

It was during the Persian rule that the king's prime minister, Haman, conceived a wicked plot to exterminate all the Jews. He surely would have succeeded except for divine intervention as recorded in the book of Esther.

Alexander was kind to the Jews. But when he died, his kingdom was divided among his four top generals who constantly fought each other for supremacy. Every time they had a war, their armies marched right through Israel. During these wars, the Jews could have been easily annihilated. But God protected them.

A descendant of one of these generals was named *Antiochus Ephiphanes.* Antiochus took control of the land of Israel, and in about the year 176 BC, he decreed that all of his subjects were to erect statues of the Greek gods, as well as himself, and worship them. His motive for doing this was to unite the empire in his struggle against the Romans. To keep the peace, some of the Jews went along with this decree while others resisted.

Determined to wipe out this resistance, Antiochus cruelly massacred tens of thousands of Jews and forbade them to practice their Judaism. To make matters worse, he erected a statue of Jupiter in the temple at Jerusalem and sacrificed a pig on the altar. This pushed the Jews, who were no longer worshiping physical idols, beyond their limit, and open conflict broke out. Although greatly outnumbered and once again threatened with annihilation, God gave the Jews a military victory sparing them from extinction.

Next came the Romans. The Roman army was the largest the world had ever known. They could easily crush any foe. And as we've just learned, they devastated the Jews in 70 and 135 AD. Well over a million Jews were killed. Those who were not killed in battle were either sold into slavery, forced to fight wild beasts in Roman arenas or tortured in other ways. Hundreds were crucified every day. The dead bodies were left to rot in the streets as a warning to any other group who was thinking about rebelling.

Every Jew the Romans could find was either killed, enslaved or exiled. *From that time until 1948 when Israel became a nation, the Jews have been wandering in exile and persecution with only the hand of God miraculously preserving them.*

Christendom And The Jews

In the second and third centuries, both Jews and Christians alike were persecuted by the Romans. But something happened that changed this—at least for the Christians. In the year 312 AD, the Roman Emperor Constantine declared Christianity to be the official religion of Rome. Except for a brief period under Julian the Apostate (360-363 AD), this brought an end to the persecution of the Christians by the Roman government.

This was certainly a welcome change. But unfortunately, it had a devasting effect on the purity of the church. Here is what happened. *The church became flooded with nonbelievers who embraced the Christian faith but never received Jesus personally as their Lord and Savior.* They outwardly professed to be Christians in order to gain favor with the Emperor and advance themselves in the Roman world. So they were Christians in name only. Many people are like that today.

This changed the nature and whole character of the church. *These nonbelievers brought their hate against the*

Jews with them into this new Christian faith. It was only a matter of time until it was manifested by anti-Jewish declarations and actions from the Roman church and government which were essentially one and the same. During this fourth century, relations between the Christian religious organization and the Jews began to deteriorate. They finally broke in the fifth century with the Roman church and government viewing the Jews as second-class citizens who were to be forever marked and branded as outcasts from the normal order and decencies of society. This policy laid the foundation for the future of the Jews as they would experience unbelievable suffering and persecution for the next 1500 years—yet survive!

As the Christian faith spread, more and more countries came under the influence of the Roman church. However, as with Rome, many people in these countries accepted the Christian faith without accepting Jesus personally and experiencing new life in Him. All they really had was religion. They continued the anti-Jewish attitudes and policies that came out of the Roman world. And the Jews, falsely believing that all Gentiles were Christians, erroneously thought that followers of Jesus were their persecutors.

We have this same problem today. The Pope recently gave an audience to Yasser Arafat. Yasser Arafat has one goal in life—to kill every Jew he can. So what do you believe the Jews will think when they see the head of the Roman church embrace the man who is committed to their destruction? They will obviously think that Christians are their enemies too. They cannot distinguish between religious organizations that are supposed to represent Christ and true individual Christians who love them.

The Crusades

One of the darkest hours for the Jews was during the period of the *Crusades.* The Crusades were military expeditions conducted under the authority and with the blessings of the Church for the purpose of recovering the Holy Land from the Moslems. These "Christian" crusades took place during the eleventh, twelfth and thirteenth centuries.

Although I'm sure some number of the Crusaders were sincere (but misguided) Christians, many more were these same evil-hearted men who were Christian in name only, seeking an opportunity to kill and plunder with impunity. They not only hated the Moslems, but they also hated the Jews. During their conquest of the holy land, they savagely butchered hundreds of thousands of Jews. *This was all done under the "banner of the cross and in the name of Christ."*

Anti-Semitism

It was also in the twelfth century that a new charge was leveled against the Jews. This was the charge of *ritual murder*. The charge was that each year at Passover, the Jews would kill a Christian boy and use his blood in the Passover ritual. This always brought violent mob action against local Jewish communities. There were a number of other similar charges against the Jews that were related to the sacraments or ordinances of the church. These too always led to mob violence against the Jews, all in the name of Christ.

As a means of further degrading the Jew, his Gentile lords, from time to time, forced all Jews to wear badges or distinctive clothing which would readily identify them as Jews. In some countries the badge was a yellow "O" similar to the yellow star later used by the Nazi Germans.

The Jews also were forced to live in restricted areas called ghettos. This was done so that the "Christian" Gentiles would not have to come into contact with and be contaminated by these "sub-human creatures." It was this attitude that Hitler played on to justify his mass murder of the Jews.

If you think this is something from our barbaric past that can never happen again in our civilized society, then you had better think again. As I was writing this very paragraph, my eye spotted an article in the newspaper concerning the Jews in Iran. The article said that Iranian Jewish school

87

children in Tehran were being forced to wear yellow uniforms to make them easily identifiable. This action has always preceded persecution of the Jews by the government that was in charge. I'm sure in the near future you will be hearing your favorite television news reporter announce that the Iranian government has taken action against the Jewish element in its country. Approximately 60,000 Jews live in Iran. They had better leave the country as soon as possible.

As incredible as it sounds, the Jews were even blamed for the horrible plague that devastated Europe in 1347-1350. It was estimated that this plague, known as the Black Death, killed approximately one-fourth of Europe's entire population. Because the Jews practiced better hygiene, they were not as susceptible to the plague as the Gentiles.

The people, needing to have someone to blame for their torment, turned their wrath against the Jews. They accused the Jews of poisoning the wells. Unruly mobs were turned loose on the Jews. Before the plague ended, thousands of Jews were killed and hundreds of Jewish communities completely annihilated.

The Inquisition

Next came the *Inquisition*. If you are an American, you remember 1492 as the year that Columbus discovered our great country. But something else happened that year which you may not have learned about in school.

The Spanish Inquisition (fifteenth and sixteenth century) was one of the most terrible periods in all of Church history. During this period, the leaders of the "Christian" religion tortured and murdered tens of thousands of true Christians who were falsely accused of being heretics. But in their passion for blood, the inquisitors also insanely killed hundreds of thousands of Jews. Again, this was all done in the name of Christ. Are you beginning to see why the Jews are intimidated by the name of Christ and feel threatened by "so-called" Christians?

The inquisition was especially perilous for the Jews in

Spain and Portugal. While Columbus was discovering America, Ferdinand and Isabella, at the insistence of the Church, began a systematic scheme which brought great suffering on the Jews. They gave the Jews the choice of forced baptism (which is no baptism at all) or exile. If they refused to be baptized, their property was confiscated and sold to the highest bidder. Perhaps it was these funds which Ferdinand and Isabella used to finance Columbus' trip? The Jews were either then killed or forced to leave the country in conditions that only the hardiest survived. *And of course the Jews associated this persecution with Christianity.*

The Russian Pogrom

As we continue on in this broad sweep of Jewish history, we come to the latter period of the nineteenth century. The setting is in eastern Europe. Millions of Jews had earlier fled there from the west to escape persecution. Poland became a refuge for them. They found favor with the Polish rulers who gave them some measure of autonomy and enabled them to live without the constant threat of persecution. The Jews felt safe, and old fears began to wane.

But the trail of tears was not over for them. Russia began to flex her muscles and conquer border states including parts of Poland, Rumania and other eastern European countries where there were large Jewish communities. Russia suddenly found herself with an unwanted population of millions of Jews.

Following the example of previous nations, Russian leaders used the Jews as a scapegoat for their internal difficulties. Their solution to this "Jewish problem" was forced conversion for one-third, emigration for another third and starvation for the last third. The Russian word *"pogrom"*, which means destruction, was the name given to this formal persecution against the Jews. This is incredible, seeing that Karl Marx, the father of communism, was a Jew. The Jews fled back to the west right into Hitler's ovens.

The Holocaust

"The final solution of the Jewish problem!" That's what Hitler called it. The Jews call it the *"holocaust!"* This was Hitler's plan for mass murder as the means to completely exterminate the Jews from the face of the earth. He almost did it. But God had promised to preserve a remnant.

Germany had been devastated by World War I. They needed someone to blame for all their problems. Hitler pointed to the Jew. He began organized persecution against them immediately after he took office in 1933. Christians and Jews alike were herded into concentration camps. In 1939, these concentration camps were turned in to *"death camps."*

As Hitler expanded his rule throughout Europe, he shipped Jews by the trainloads from their homelands to these camps. These death factories were so efficient that some of them could mass murder 25,000 human beings every day.

The Jews were stripped of their clothes and herded into gas chambers they thought were shower rooms. When the room was full, the doors were shut, and the people were gassed to death. Afterwards, workers removed gold teeth and wedding rings to be melted down into gold bars. Women's hair was cut off and used in the manufacture of cloth and mattresses. Body fat was used to make inexpensive soap. The after the bodies were cremated, the ashes were used for fertilizer.

The Jewish population in Europe in 1939 was about nine million. Hitler reduced it to about three million. The horror of the holocaust finally awakened the Jew to the fact that the world did not want him. There was no place safe for him to live except in his own homeland. As horrible as this demonic-inspired torture was, God used it to put the desire in the Jewish heart to return to his ancient land in fulfillment of Bible prophecy and God's plan for Israel.

In this brief survey of Jewish history, we've seen how one would-be world ruler after another has tried to wipe the Jewish people off the face of the earth. They and their king-

90

doms have come and gone. Yet the Jews have survived. And today, after two thousand years of exile, they are back in their land and rapidly becoming one of the most powerful nations of the world. How can this be? There's only one answer. You ask me to show you one verse in the Bible to prove that it's true? I'll show you one word—the *"Jew!"*

Scripture References

Some Scriptures where God said He would preserve a remnant of the Jews are given below:

"And for those who are left alive, I will cause them to be dragged away to distant lands as prisoners of war, and slaves. There they will live in constant fear. The sound of a leaf driven in the wind will send them fleeing as though chased by a man with a sword; they shall fall when no one is pursuing them. Yes, though none pursue them they shall stumble over each other in flight, as though fleeing in battle, with no power to stand before their enemies. You shall perish among the nations and be destroyed among your enemies. Those left shall pine away in enemy lands because of their sins, the same sins as those of their fathers.

"But despite all they have done, I will not utterly destroy them and my covenant with them, for I am Jehovah their God" (Leviticus 26:36-39, 44 TLB).

"Yet a tenth—a remnant—will survive; and though Israel is invaded again and again and destroyed, yet Israel will live like a tree cut down, whose stump still lives to grow again" (Isaiah 6:13 TLB).

"At that time the Lord will bring back a remnant of his people for the second time, returning them to the land of Israel. . .He will raise a flag among the nations for them to rally to; he will gather the scattered Israelites from the ends of the earth" (Isaiah 11:11-12 TLB).

"The Lord's decree of desolation covers all the land.

'Yet,' he says, 'there will be a little remnant of my people left" (Jeremiah 4:27 TLB).

"But I will not completely blot you out. So says the Lord" (Jeremiah 5:18 TLB).

"So don't be afraid, O Jacob my servant; don't be dismayed, O Israel; for I will bring you home again from distant lands, and your children from your exile. They shall have rest and quiet in their own land, and no one shall make them afraid. For I am with you and I will save you, says the Lord. Even if I utterly destroy the nations where I scatter you, I will not exterminate you; I will punish you, yes—you will not go unpunished" (Jeremiah 30:10-11 TLB).

"Fear not, O Jacob, my servant, says the Lord, for I am with you. I will destroy all the nations to which I have exiled you, but I will not destroy you. I will punish you, but only enough to correct you" (Jeremiah 46:28 TLB).

"But I will spare a few of them from death by war and famine and disease. I will save them to confess to the nations how wicked they have been, and they shall know I am the Lord" (Ezekiel 12:16 TLB).

Chapter 10—God Will Preserve A Remnant

Study Guide 9

1. Describe the conflict between the Jews and Antiochus Epiphanes.

   Antiochus pieced pagan Idols and some Jews served them. But when he sacrificed a pig. Many jews got very mad.

2. Explain what change took place in the Christian religion that allowed the institutional church to persecute the Jews.

   Constantine declared Christianity the official religion of Rome.

3. Briefly define the following terms:

   a. Crusades - *Butchers of moslems + jews to regain the holy land.*

   b. Inquisition - *Persecution of true Christians and forced Baptism of Jews. (Robbery)*

   c. Holocaust - *Hitlers plan to elliminate the "problem" of the Jews.*

11

God Will Bring The Jews Back To Their Land

Perhaps the most significant event of modern times is the rebirth of the nation of Israel. Just think of it! After all these centuries, the Jews are back in their own land. There is no other possible explanation for this incredible fact except the biblical one.

The man whom God used to promote this return was *Theodore Herzl.* Herzl was born in 1860 in Budapest. He was the son of a wealthy banker. Herzl himself studied law but later became a journalist. He was well assimilated into the Gentile world in which he lived and felt very comfortable in it. He believed that modern man had become so civilized and tolerant of his fellowman, that Gentile prejudices against Jews would soon disappear.

But in 1894, Herzl had an experience that showed him the

foolishness of his logic and his total ignorance of men's hearts. This experience became known as the *"Dreyfus Affair."*

Alfred Dreyfus was a captain in the French army and a Jew. He had been accused of giving French military secrets to the Germans and was publicly humiliated and sentenced to life imprisonment. This guilty verdict was passed even though there was little evidence to support it. During the trial, the public demanded justice. But their demands were not so much because they thought Dreyfus was a traitor, but because he was a Jew. Herzl was in Paris covering the story. As he heard the angry mobs scream, "Kill the traitor, kill the Jew," chills ran through his blood. His eyes were opened to the fact that Gentile hate of the Jews would never disappear, and, given the opportunity, they would again try to wipe them off the face of the earth.

The Birth of Zionism

Herzl's entire attitude had now changed. He saw the Jew would never be safe outside of his own land. In 1896, he wrote *The Jewish State*. In this little book, he stated the problem and challenged the Jews to work toward the establishment of their own nation. In 1897, he called together the first meeting to lay the groundwork for what would later become known as *"Zionism."* At this meeting held in Basil, Switzerland, Herzl predicted that within fifty years the Jews would have their own state.

There was only one problem with this prediction—the land of Palestine was under control of the Turks. They had ruled over this land since 1517 and were not about to give it up to a bunch of Jews. But something happened that changed the situation. That "something" was World War I.

In this terrible war, Turkey and England fought each other for control of the Middle East. England won. Ironically enough, a Jewish chemist named *Chaim Weizmann* made a major contribution to the war effort for England. He developed a means for improving the making of explosives which England vitally needed. The Prime Minister of England publicly recognized Weizmann's contribution and desired to reward him. Weizmann did not seek personal gain but instead asked that England grant the Jews a national homeland in Palestine.

The Prime Minister agreed and in 1917 the British Foreign Secretary, James Balfour, prepared a declaration that established the mandate for the Jews to once again occupy their ancient land. As horrible as the war was, God used it to bring the Jews back home for the final and complete fulfillment of the land promise He made to Abraham 4,000 years ago.

The newly formed League of Nations gave its stamp of approval to the Balfour Declaration. But except for a few religious zealots and political idealists, the Jews were not too thrilled with the idea of returning to their land. They were too comfortably assimilated in the Gentile world in which they lived. They had not been in Paris with Herzl. They had not seen what he had seen. It had been too long since they had heard "Kill the Jew—Kill the Jew!" World War II woke them up. Hitler's death camps opened their eyes to the stark reality of what Herzl saw at the Dreyfus' trial. Thus the Jews began a mass exodus back to their land.

Herzl's prediction that the Jews would have their own state within fifty years proved to be prophetic. *On November 29, 1947, the United Nations voted on what God had already decreed, and officially established the existence of the state of Israel.* They decided to partition the land into a Jewish state and an Arab state, while making Jerusalem an international city.

This plan was accepted by the Jews. The land given to them was only ten miles wide at its middle and vulnerable to attack from every side. Much of it was desert, and almost one-half of the inhabitants were Arabs. Yet the plan did establish them as an independent state. And for this the Jews rejoiced.

The Arabs were not so joyous. They resented this Jewish intrusion and rejected the plan. They felt confident they could drive the Jews into the Mediterranean Sea. In view of their superior numbers, the Arabs were more interested in a military solution to the division of the land than they were a political one. They instructed the Arabs who were living in the land to flee to the neighboring Arab countries until the Jews were annihilated. Then they could return and possess the land. *The Jews begged these Arabs to stay.*

The War of Independence

On May 14, 1948, the Jewish people declared their independence. The following day, this new state of Israel was attacked by the combined armies of Syria, Lebanon, Jordan, Egypt and Iraq. Egypt invaded from the south. Syria and Lebanon from the north. From the east came Jordan and Iraq. The Mediterranean was to the west. The Jews had their backs to the sea. There was no place to run.

The total Jewish population in the land at this time was about 650,000 men, women and children. The small Jewish militia had very little armament. What they did have was outdated. The land they had to defend was long and skinny. Most of it was borderland, surrounded on three sides by the enemy. From a military perspective, it seemed indefensible.

The total Arab population surrounding Israel was from 100 to 150 million, representing a number of different countries. The land area they occupied was two hundred times larger than that of the Jews. Their armies were well-equipped with more modern weapons. Rightly so, the Arabs were confident of a quick victory and an end to the "Jewish problem."

But God had not preserved a remnant of Jews and brought them back to the land so they could be driven into the Sea. Not only did the Jews survive and hold their ground, but they gained additional land which had not been included in the earlier proposal by the United Nations.

The Arab state which had been proposed by the United Nations never came into existence because Jordan annexed most of the territory west of the Jordan River which had been allocated to the Arabs as their state. Egypt took control of the Gaza Strip in the south which had also been allocated to the Arabs.

Neither did Jerusalem become an international city. It was divided between Israel and Jordan. Israel captured the western part of Jerusalem which was the modern section of the city. Jordan took control of the old city of Jerusalem which included the ancient temple site, the holiest place of Judaism. A no man's land was established between the divided city.

With Israel now established as a nation, Jews from all over the world began to return to their homeland. Within the next three years, the population doubled as over 700,000 Jews poured into Israel. These Jews came mainly from Europe and the Arab countries. Many thousands more came over the next few years. Sometimes entire Jewish communities packed up their bags and headed for Israel. God was bringing them home. *But would they be there to stay?*

The Sinai Campaign

The War of Independence ended in an uneasy truce. The Arab states considered themselves to be in a continual state of war against Israel. There were many border incidents, particularly from the Egyptian controlled Sinai Peninsula. Arab raiders were sent on murderous suicide missions deep into Israeli territory. Tensions mounted.

Finally in 1956, the Egyptian ruler, Abdul Nasser, seized control of the Suez Canal and prepared to attack Israel with a united Arab alliance that included Egypt, Jordan and Syria. Nasser's action to take control of the Suez Canal angered the British and French. They sought Israel's help in reopening the canal.

On October 29, 1956, Israel invaded the Sinai and quickly defeated the Egyptian forces, pushing them back to the Suez Canal. General Moshe Dayan led this 110-mile march destroying commando bases along the way. Israel took 6,000 Egyptian prisoners and huge quantities of armaments and supplies. Meanwhile, the British and French were bombing the Egyptian strongholds and taking control of the Suez Canal.

The United Nations called an emergency session to stop the fighting. With the backing of both the United States and Russia, they forced Israel and her allies to withdraw from the captured territory. United Nation observers were then stationed along the Egyptian border. *The significance of the Sinai Campaign was that it bought Israel time to develop more strongly as a nation.*

The Six Day War

For the next ten years, Israel and her Arab neighbors lived in relative peace with Arab hostilities limited to terrorist actions against Israel. During this period, Russia supplied the Arab armies with a massive amount of weapons and other military aid.

The Arabs, led by Nasser, continued their "state of war" attitude against Israel. Russia was desiring to gain influence in the Middle East and capitalize on the conflict. In 1967, Russian intelligence sent exaggerated reports to both Syria and Egypt concerning war preparations of Israel.

Nasser's popularity at home was low. He needed to reestablish his prestige as the leader of the Arab world. The only way he could do that would be to defeat Israel. With encouragement from the Russians, he again made an alliance with Syria and Jordan to destroy Israel. *The stated Arab goal was not only to defeat the Israeli military and reclaim the land, but to kill every Jew alive—man, woman and child.* But God had different plans.

In May, 1967, Nasser began to move his troops into the Sinai. He ordered the United Nations peace-keeping force out of the area. Then as a final attempt to provoke Israel, he blocked the Israeli port of Eilat on the Gulf of Aquaba.

Israel was left with no choice but to retaliate. On the 5th of June, 1967, Israel made a lightning attack against her enemies. Israeli jets, flying low to avoid radar, swept into Egypt from the Mediterranean and totally destroyed the entire Egyptian air force. The results were the same against

Jordan and Syria. Well over four hundred Russian supplied Arab planes were destroyed on their airfields before the pilots could ever get them off the ground.

The Egyptian ground force in the Sinai was also routed. The Israelis destroyed 600 to 700 Russian supplied tanks and captured more than one hundred tanks that were undamaged. In addition, they took huge quantities of weapons of various types and much other military equipment.

Weapons were not all they took. They also captured Arab land. *The longer the Arabs persisted in fighting, the more land they lost.* By the time the war was over, Israel occupied the Sinai Peninsula and the Gaza Strip, from which Egypt had made many raids into Israel. For years, Syria had fired on Israeli civilians from the strategic area of the Golan Heights. Now it was occupied by Israel. Jordan had used the West Bank (the biblical land area of Judea and Samaria) for similar terrorist activities. It too fell into Israeli hands. Incredibly, the war was over in just six days.

Perhaps the most important outcome of this was the Israeli occupation of the old city of Jerusalem which they took from Jordan. The Jews had not been masters of Jerusalem since 606 BC when Nebuchadnezzar conquered it. They had been banned from living there since 135 AD by the Romans. Now after all these centuries, the Jews were back in their land and in possession of their ancient capital city. *Could this be in preparation for the coming of their Messiah?*

The Yom-Kippur War

The Arab world was humiliated by the stunning defeat. Nasser blamed the loss on British and American support for Israel—an accusation he dreamed up to save face. Arab pride had been devastated. They felt a desperate need to regain their self-respect as well as recover territory lost to Israel. They again looked to Russia for military assistance. Russia eagerly rearmed them and a massive military build up took place.

The Arabs began the fourth round of war on the Jewish

most holy day—Yom Kippur. The invasion took place on October 6, 1973. Most Jews on that day were in the synagogues observing their religious practices. The nation was not properly prepared. They had purposefully let the Arabs make the first move in order not to be criticized as the aggressor.

Egypt crossed the Suez Canal and attacked the Sinai while Syria simultaneously invaded the Golan Heights. Other Arab countries joined the attack. For the first few days, the Arabs had the advantage. But as the war progressed, the superior Israeli military forces turned the momentum to their favor.

On the northern front, the Israelis pushed back the Syrians and advanced to within twenty miles of Damascus. To the south, they had successfully crossed the Suez Canal and had surrounded the entire Egyptian third army which was trapped in the Sinai. This was about twenty thousand soldiers. The Israelis could have easily conquered them.

Once again the United Nations and the superpowers intervened to stop the war. The United States secretary of state, Henry Kessinger, negotiated a "separation of forces" between Israel and Egypt. This saved the Egyptian Third Army from complete destruction. A similar agreement was made with Syria. Thus, once again we see God supernaturally protected His covenant people and gave them victory over their enemies. *The significance of this war was that the Arabs regained some self-respect and the Jews began to sense the divine protection of God.*

The Invasion Of Lebanon

At the time of this writing, the current crisis in the Middle East is concerned with the Israeli invasion of Lebanon and the PLO. *Why did Israel feel it was necessary to invade Lebanon? And who are the PLO? Let's begin with the PLO.*

As we've just learned, when Israel declared her independence in 1948, the Arabs who were living in the land were told by their leaders to flee until they drove Israel into the Sea. Then they could return and possess the land. *These*

102

Arabs are called Palestinians because Palestine is the name of the land area in which they were living. Remember, the Roman Emperor Hadrian gave the land this name. Many of these Arabs fled to Jordan and Lebanon.

Since the Arabs expected to return the Palestinians to the land, they did not really assimilate them into their country. Instead, they placed them in refugee camps. With each successive Israeli victory, the number of Arabs leaving Israel grew from 150,000 to over 600,000. *The Arab countries refused to take them in as citizens and care for their needs. Instead, they used them as political pawns in their continuing struggle against Israel and their ambition to establish a Palestinian state.*

With each Israeli victory, it became more and more clear that the Arab nations were not going to defeat Israel. In view of this, a small group of terrorists organized and called themselves the Palestine Liberation Organization (PLO). *The PLO is a terrorist organization formed for the sole purpose of destroying the nation of Israel.* They appointed themselves as leaders of the displaced Palestinian refugees. The Arab nations use the PLO as their means for unofficially carrying out their continued war against Israel.

The PLO initially made their headquarters in Jordan. Yasser Arafat became their leader. By using force and the rule of the gun, the PLO took over the refugee camps in Jordan. Through fear and intimidation, they turned these refugee camps into military strongholds from which they conducted raids into Israel.

In September, 1970, the PLO tried to overthrow Jordan's King Hussein. King Hussein defeated them, killing 10,000 Palestinians, and the PLO fled to Lebanon, where they infiltrated and took control of the refugee camps there. By then the number of refugees had grown to several hundred thousand. The PLO organized and indoctrinated the young Arab males into their growing militia. With money from Saudia Arabia, they were able to purchase arms from Russia and other countries who wanted to see Israel destroyed. Their terrorist organization was growing into a small, well-equipped army.

Unlike Jordan, Lebanon did not have a strong central government. They couldn't stop the PLO from taking over the southern part of the country. The PLO was rapidly becoming a state within a state. In 1975, they began a civil war against the Lebanese Christians. These Lebanese Christians were called Phalangists. *In the next seven years, over 100,000 Lebanese were brutally massacred by the PLO—not Israel.*

In an effort to end the bloodshed, the United Nations allowed Syria to send "peace-keeping" forces into Lebanon. Syria had been wanting to take over Lebanon for years. They saw this as their opportunity. The Syrian President, Hafez Assad, moved 30,000 troops into Lebanon. He also put missiles in the Bekaa Valley. But instead of being a peacemaker, the Syrians gave the PLO a free hand in butchering the Christians and shelling Israel's northern cities.

As the attacks on Israel increased, it became clear that they could no longer tolerate the situation. Finally on June 5, 1982, Israel invaded southern Lebanon for the purpose of eliminating the PLO strongholds and liberating Lebanon from their oppressors. Syria responded to this invasion with an air attack. Incredibly, Israel destroyed eighty-two Russian supplied Syrian planes without losing a single one themselves.

Israel also captured a staggering amount of arms Russia had supplied to the PLO. Some reports said that there were enough military supplies stashed in the mountains to equip an army of several hundred thousand. This was certainly far beyond what was needed by the PLO. It was also revealed that approximately one-half of the PLO were not even Palestinians. They were paid mercenaries from communist controlled countries.

Russia's clear intention was to arm these forces and use them to wipe out Israel so that they could take control of the Middle East. But this didn't happen. And it's not going to happen. One day in the near future Russia will realize that none of her hired hands can defeat Israel. She will then make the fatal mistake of trying it herself.

The Coming War With Russia

One of the next major events to take place in our world in fulfillment of God's plan for Israel is the Russian invasion of the Middle East. One doesn't have to be a Bible scholar to realize their present threat to world peace. Yet the prophet Ezekiel predicted this ominous event a long time ago while he was a captive in Babylon (about 575 BC). His prediction is preserved for us in Ezekiel 38-39. It would be helpful for you to read these two chapters.

The first question we need to ask ourselves after reading Ezekiel's prophecy is, "What makes us think Ezekiel is speaking about Russia?" After all, Russia didn't even exist in his day. As we carefully observe Ezekiel's prophecy, we discover four reasons that clearly lead us to believe he was talking about modern Russia.

The first reason has to do with the names that Ezekiel mentions. In Genesis 10, we find a list of the ancient nations of the world as they descended from Noah's sons. The key names in Ezekiel's prophecy are mentioned. Historians and Bible scholars have traced the migration of these people and discovered that they and their descendants settled in the geographic area we know today as Russia and Eastern Europe. Their names have changed over the centuries, but the geographic location is the same.

A second reason we are led to believe this is Russia is *the time* when Ezekiel says this nation will be in power. He says that God will make this nation powerful and pull her into the Middle East in the "latter years" (Ezekiel 38:8). He further emphasizes the timing of this event by saying it will be in the "latter days" (Ezekiel 38:16). These are key phrases in the Bible that refer to the end-times just prior to the coming of Messiah Jesus to planet earth. Thus this nation would have to be a world power at this point in time and history. Russia, as we know her today, did not even exist before the twentieth century and has only become a world power in the last thirty years.

A third reason we are convinced this is Russia is in regard to its relationship to the establishment of the *state of Israel*. Ezekiel says this was will not take place until the Jews are back in their own land (Ezekiel 38:8,12). As we've learned in this chapter, the state of Israel didn't come into existence until 1948. Therefore, Ezekiel's prediction could not have been fulfilled before then. Ironically, Russia's massive military buildup has coincided with the establishment and growth of the state of Israel. God is preparing them to make a military venture into the Middle East to fulfill this ancient propecy.

Finally, we are led to believe this is Russia because of its *geographic location*. Three times Ezekiel identifies this invading country as being to the north of Israel (Ezekiel 38:6,15; 39:2). Russia is the only great power to the north of Israel. And if you'll look on a map, you'll notice that Moscow is almost perfectly due north of Jerusalem. Isn't that incredible!

So yes, Russia is going to invade the Middle East and trigger World War III. She'll have a number of allies who will join her in this venture. But God will not allow Russia to destroy Israel. Instead, God Himself will destroy Russia. Ezekiel predicted that God would fight against Russia with great earthquakes, plagues, torrential rains, hailstorms, fire and brimstone, and the firepower of Israel's allies (Ezekiel 38:18-23). My point here is not to go into the details of this war. Many good books have been written on this subject. I am simply pointing out that it is going to happen as part of God's plan for Israel.

Ezekiel says that God will destroy 85 percent of the Russian army, along with her allies (Ezekiel 39:2). They will never reach Jerusalem. The destruction will be so bad that it will take seven months just to bury the dead (Ezekiel 39:12). The result of this war is that God will be glorified and the nation of Israel will once again begin to turn her heart toward God (Ezekiel 39:21-29).

To summarize, we see that God used World War I to pre-pare the land, freeing it from Turkish rule. He used the hor-ror of World War II to prepare the people to return to the land so He can make them a great nation. He is going to use World War III to prepare the Jewish heart to receive their Messiah. Then His ancient promise to Abraham will be ful-filled at the return of Messiah Jesus.

Scripture References

There are many Scriptures that speak of God bringing the Jews back to their land. A few of these are as follows:

"When all these things have happened to you—the blessings and the curses I have listed—you will medi-tate upon them as you are living among the nations where the Lord your God will have driven you. If at that time you want to return to the Lord your God and you and your children have begun wholeheartedly to obey all of the commandments I have given you today, then the Lord your God will rescue you from your cap-tivity! He will have mercy upon you and come and gather you out of all the nations where he will have scattered you. Though you are at the ends of the earth, he will go and find you and bring you back again to the land of your ancestors. You shall possess the land again, and he will do you good and bless you even more than he did your ancestors" (Deuteronomy 30:1-5 TLB).

"So don't be afraid, O Jacob my servant; don't be dis-mayed, O Israel; for I will bring you home again from distant lands, and your children from their exile. They shall have rest and quiet in their own land, and no one shall make them afraid. For I am with you and I will save you, says the Lord. Even if I utterly destroy the nations where I scatter you, I will not exterminate you; I will punish you, yes—you will not go unpunished" (Jeremiah 30:10-11 TLB).

"Listen to this message from the Lord, you nations of

the world, and publish it abroad: The Lord who scattered his people will gather them back together again and watch over them as a shepherd does his flock. He will save Israel from those who are too strong for them" (Jeremiah 31:10-11 TLB).

"But tell the exiles that the Lord God says: Although I have scattered you in the countries of the world, yet I will be a sanctuary to you for the time that you are there, and I will gather you back from the nations where you are scattered and give you the land of Israel again" (Ezekiel 11:16-17 TLB).

"For the Lord God says: I will search and find my sheep. I will be like a shepherd looking for his flock. I will find my sheep and rescue them from all the places they were scattered in that dark and cloudy day. And I will bring them back from among the people and nations where they were, back home to their own land of Israel. . ." (Ezekiel 34:11-13 TLB).

"Son of dust, when the people of Israel were living in their own country, they defiled it by their evil deeds; to me their worship was as foul as filthy rags. They polluted the land with murder and with the worshiping of idols, so I poured out my fury upon them. And I exiled them to many lands. But when they were scattered out among the nations, then they were a blight upon my holy name because the nations said, 'These are the people of God and he couldn't protect them from harm!' I am concerned about my reputation that was ruined by my people through the world.

Therefore say to the people of Israel: The Lord God says, I am bringing you back again, but not because you deserve it; I am doing it to protect my holy name which you tarnished among the nations. I will honor my great name that you defiled, and the people of the world shall know I am the Lord. I will be honored before their eyes by delivering you from exile among them. For I will bring you back home again to the land of Israel" (Ezekiel 36:16-24 TLB).

"These bones," he said, "represent all the people of Israel. They say: 'We have become a heap of dried-out bones—all hope is gone.' But tell them, the Lord God says: My people, I will open your graves of exile and cause you to rise again and return to the land of Israel. And, then at last, O my people, you will know I am the Lord.

For the Lord God says: I am gathering the people of Israel from among the nations, and bringing them home from around the world to their own land, to unify them into one nation" (Ezekiel 37:11-13, 21-22 TLB).

"I will restore the fortunes of my people Israel, and they shall rebuild their ruined cities, and live in them again, and they shall plant vineyards and gardens and eat their crops and drink their wine. I will firmly plant them there upon the land that I have given them; they shall not be pulled up again". . . (Amos 9:14-15 TLB).

"At that time, I will gather you together and bring you home again, and give you a good name, a name of distinction among all the peoples of the earth, and they will praise you when I restore your fortunes before your very eyes," says the Lord" (Zephaniah 3:20 TLB).

Chapter 11—God Will Bring The Jews Back To Their Land

Study Guide 10

1. State what Herzl experienced that changed his attitude toward the Jews having their own land.

   The trial of Dryfus in France "Dryfus Affair"

2. Briefly state the main significance of the following wars:

   a. War of Independence - *The victory was supernatural. The Jews were greatly outnumbered.*

   b. Sinai Campaign - *Control of Suez Canal. Israel developed more strongly as a nation*

   c. Six Day War - *Clean sweep of Nasser. Israeli occupation of Jerusalem*

   d. Yom-Kippur War - *Jews sensed divine protection of God*

   e. Lebanon Invasion - *Russia's Paid mercenaries*

   f. Russian Invasion - *Fulfilment of Ezekiels prophesy.*

12

The Jews Will Go Through Tribulation

We are seeing very clearly how God has literally fulfilled the first seven points of Moses' prophecy. In this and the following chapters, we're going to turn our attention to the last three points that are yet to be fulfilled in the future.

But first, I would like to bring to your attention the following thought—*since these first seven points have been literally fulfilled just as Moses predicted, doesn't it seem likely that these last three points will also be fulfilled?* The obvious answer is "yes," because Moses was speaking under the inspiration of God. There is no other explanation. Let's now see what he says about God's plan for Israel in the future.

The persecution the Jewish people have experienced the last 2,000 years has been horrifying. I wish I could say it was over. But unfortunately the worst is yet to come. Moses

111

predicted that the Jews would go through *"tribulation."* We've been learning in the previous chapters that they have already gone through tribulation. No other ethnic group of people have suffered like the Jews. But there's more to come. In fact, the persecution the Jews will experience in the near future will be the worst they have ever known. It makes me sick to think about it, but the coming tribulation for the Jewish people will far exceed even the holocaust.

The Jews' Final Holocaust

What is this terrible tribulation that awaits the Jews? Moses said it would take place in the *"latter days."* It is the last seven years of this age just prior to the coming of Messiah Jesus to earth. The Bible says this will be a time of suffering such as the world has never known. The last three and one-half years of this period will be so bad that Jesus referred to it as the "great tribulation" (Matthew 24:21).

The purpose of this tribulation period is to prepare the world for the return of Messiah Jesus to rule the earth, not only as King of the Jews, but also as King of kings and Lord of lords.

This involves God dealing with both the Jews and the Gentiles. For the Jews, God will use this period of tribulation as the final preparation of the nation of Israel to acknowledge and receive Jesus as their Messiah. As we have seen, God has preserved the Jewish people throughout history. There will be a remnant of Jews who will accept Jesus as their Messiah and enter into the covenant blessings promised through Abraham. To the Gentiles, the tribulation period will be a time of God pouring out His holy wrath against their unrighteousness and for the way they have treated Israel. God's wrath against sin will be manifested in His judgements on mankind as described in the book of Revelation (chapters 6-19).

The world does not believe that Messiah Jesus is coming. The world does not expect Messiah Jesus to come. The world does not want Messiah Jesus to come. But He is com-

ing. And the tribulation period is necessary to prepare the unbelieving world for it.

Many people think the world is going to end when Messiah Jesus comes. But the world is not going to end. What is going to end is the present age in which we live. But first, this present world order must come to an end. It must come to an end because it is an anti-God system. The tribulation period will bring it to an end. Then Messiah Jesus will come and establish a new world order based on justice and righteousness. Let's now take a closer look at this tribulation that lies ahead for the Jewish people.

The Antichrist

The tribulation period begins when Israel signs a peace treaty with the one we know of as the Antichrist (Daniel 9;27;Isaiah 28:18). This treaty is supposed to be for seven years, but as we'll see in this chapter it will be broken in the middle of the seven years. The word Antichrist not only means one who is against Christ but also one who takes the place of Christ. *The Antichrist will deceive the world into believing that he is the Christ who can solve the world's problems and bring peace among the nations, particularly the Middle East* (1 Thessalonians 5:3).

It seems that the Antichrist will be the leader of a one-world government that has its power centered in a ten-nation western confederacy. We might think of this ten-nation confederacy as the United States of Europe. He will be a very persuasive person who will be able to unite this western confederacy into a common political, military and economic system that will dominate the world.

The world is now looking for such a person whom they think can solve the complex problems of our day. Every nation is rapidly becoming an armed camp. More and more countries have the bomb. East and West can't seem to work out their differences. Both are preparing for war. The Middle East is a powder keg. Nuclear holocaust seems inevitable. Political unrest is at an all time high. Revolution is the byword of the day. Anarchy and lawlessness is the rule.

113

Entire nations are on the verge of bankruptcy. Worldwide economic disaster waits just around the corner. Resources are being used up faster than we can replace them. Immorality is rampant. Societies are falling apart. Religious institutions are helpless bystanders. Scientists, educators and technocrats realize they can't solve the world's problems. World events are out of control and seem to be racing to a catastrophic end. *If someone can step onto center stage of the world scene and promise to solve all these problems, the world will certainly acknowledge him as their leader. This someone is the Antichrist.*

A False Peace

The Antichrist will develop a peace plan for the Middle East to which Israel and her Arab neighbors will agree. It will guarantee Israel secure borders and allow the religious leaders of Israel to rebuild their ancient temple. This will enable them to once again make sacrifices as they did before the Romans destroyed the temple and scattered them as a nation. The Antichrist will dominate the nations of the world, seem to bring peace to the Middle East and make it possible for the Jews to practice their ancient religion. For these reasons, many of the Jewish people will accept the Antichrist as a kind of Messiah.

The nation of Israel will believe that she has finally entered into her golden age of which the prophets spoke and for which she has been waiting for centuries. But it is a terrible deception. The Antichrist will become drunk with power. He will have a religious counterpart whom the Bible calls the False Prophet (Revelation 16:13; 19:20; 20:10). The False Prophet will be the leader of the one-world religious system that will come to power along with the Antichrist. *The False Prophet will be able to unite all the religions of the world into a single organizational structure just as the Antichrist will unite the political, military and economic systems.*

The Abomination of Desolation

In order to establish more complete authority and control for the Antichrist, the False Prophet will devise a scheme which will require everyone to acknowledge the Antichrist as being divine—that is, God Himself in their midst. This will be a type of emperor worship.

People will acknowledge their worship of the Antichrist by taking his mark in their right hand or in their forehead (Revelation 13:11-18). This mark will identify individuals with the Antichrist and will be a visible sign of their complete allegiance to him. No one will be able to work or conduct any kind of business unless they have this mark. *The Bible warns people not to be deceived by the Antichrist nor take his mark* (Revelation 14:9-11; 16:2; 19:20). However, the unbelieving world will be deceived by their hard hearts and do so anyway, thus sealing their eternal damnation (2 Thessalonians 2:9-12; Revelation 13:4).

This plan of giving worship to the Antichrist will be put into effect at the middle of the seven-year peace treaty with Israel (Daniel 9:24-27). As part of the plan, the False Prophet will erect an image of the Antichrist in the holy of holies in the rebuilt temple at Jerusalem. This is the most sacred place in their midst, as recorded in the Bible.

Because of what the Antichrist will have done for the nation of Israel, he fully expects the Jews to worship him. The False Prophet will convince him that they will. Some will, but most won't. To the average Jew, placing an image of a man in the holy of holies to be worshiped is the worst possible offense to their religious beliefs. The prophet Daniel and Jesus spoke of this as the abomination of desolation (Daniel 9:27; 12:11; Matthew 24:15). The apostle Paul also referred to this event, as did John in the book of Revelation (2 Thessalonians 2:4; Revelation 13:14-15).

By this time hundreds of thousands of Jews will have come to accept Jesus as their Messiah. This will come about through the preaching ministry of 144,000 Jewish evangelists whom God will call especially for the purpose of preaching the gospel during the tribulation period (Revelation 7:1-

8; 14:1-5). These followers of Jesus will know the Antichrist is not the Messiah. They will refuse to worship him and take his mark. In addition, many Jews will have become devoutly religious, even though they will not have yet acknowledged Jesus as their Messiah. They too will refuse to worship the Antichrist.

The Great Tribulation

The Antichrist will not take this rejection kindly. He will have done much for Israel, and he will see this as ingratitude on their part. *In view of this, he will seek to kill every Jew and rid himself and the world of these problem people once and for all.* Thus will begin the greatest period of tribulation the Jews have ever known in their long history of suffering and persecution. This is the time Moses was predicting would come about in his sermon in Deuteronomy. It is also the time that Jesus warned the Jews about in the 24th chapter of Matthew.

The Antichrist will march his troops into Israel and for a short period of time will occupy Jerusalem (Zechariah 14:2; Luke 21:24; Revelation 11:2). *Every nation will support his retaliation against Israel for their disturbing world peace* (Zechariah 12:2-3, 9; 14:2; Joel 3:2; Isaiah 66:18). The Antichrist will kill two-thirds of all the Jews (Zechariah 13:8). This could mean that up to ten million Jews will be killed. The Antichrist will plunder the beloved city of Jerusalem, and one-half of the citizens will be forced into exile (Zechariah 14:2).

Jesus warned the Jews to flee Jerusalem when they see the Antichrist set up his image in the temple (Matthew 24:15-21). They will run to the hills of Judea and down to the Dead Sea region where there are many caves in which they will be able to hide (Luke 21:21).

Many Bible students believe a considerable number of the Jews will find refuge in the ancient rock city of Petra. Petra is located in Jordan just south of the Dead Sea. It is situated in a canyon with high cliffs and only one narrow

116

entrance way. These cliffs almost come together at the top making Petra a natural bombshelter.

The Antichrist will pursue these Jews who will have fled for their lives. But God will hinder him from catching up to them and protect them for the next three and one-half years (Revelation 12). This will make the Antichrist furious. He will then turn and seek to kill the rest of the Jews who were not able to flee the city.

The prophet Daniel says the Antichrist will kill many of the Jewish believers in Jesus who have refused to worship him (Daniel 7:25; 12:7). The book of Revelation confirms this mass murder of Jewish believers (Revelation 12:11,17). The Antichrist will also seek to kill all Christians because they will be in sympathy with the Jews and will have also refused to worship him and take his mark. Many will be killed (Revelation 7:9-17).

During this time of trouble, God will raise up two Jewish prophets in Jerusalem who will point many of the devout Jews to Jesus as their Messiah (Revelation 11:3-13). They will preach under the protection of God so that the Antichrist will not be able to harm them. God will give them supernatural power to do many signs and wonders.

When their ministry to their Jewish brethren is over, God will allow the Antichrist to kill them. As a way of gloating over their death, the Antichrist will put their bodies on display for three and one-half days. The whole world will view these lifeless bodies and celebrate the Antichrist's victory over them.

But their celebration will be shortlived. At the end of the three and one-half days, God will resurrect these two prophets and catch them up to heaven. Immediately a great earthquake will level one-tenth of Jerusalem leaving 7,000 dead. The result will be that more devout Jews will turn to Jesus as their Messiah.

In the meantime, God will be pouring out His judgements against the Antichrist and the nations of the world. The book of Revelation describes these judgements in terms of seals, trumpets, and vials (bowls). I believe these divine

117

judgements follow one another in a chronological sequence with each series of judgements being more intense than the preceding ones. These judgements reveal the wrath of God from heaven against the Antichrist and all peoples who have taken his mark. (See Revelation 6,8,9,16.)

The tribulation period will be a time of suffering greater than the world has ever known. Jesus said that the entire human race would be destroyed except this period be cut short by His own return to planet earth in fulfillment of God's promise to Abraham (Matthew 24:22).

He also said the generation that will be alive when these events take place will live to see the coming of the Messiah. For my Jewish friends who must endure these hardships, take courage and lift your heads to heaven for your redemption draws near.

As terrifying as this period will be, God will use it to work in the Jewish heart a true repentance and desire to return to God. This will lead them to acknowledge Jesus as their Messiah and pray for His coming to deliver them from their enemies and to be their King.

Scripture References

The following are just a few Scriptures that predict this most terrible time of suffering for the Jewish people:

"When you are in tribulation, and all these things come upon you in the latter days" (Deuteronomy 4:30 RSV).

"Alas, in all history when has there ever been a time of terror such as in that coming day? It is a time of trouble for my people—for Jacob—such as they have never known before. Yet God will rescue them" (Jeremiah 30:7 TLB).

"AT THAT time Michael, the mighty angelic prince who stands guard over your nation, will stand up (and fight for you in heaven against satanic forces), and there will be a time of anguish for the Jews greater than any previous suffering in Jewish history. And yet every one of your people whose names are written in the Book will endure it" (Daniel 12:1 TLB).

"He (Antichrist) will defy the Most High God, and wear down the saints with persecution. . ." (Daniel 7:25 TLB).

"Two thirds of all the nation of Israel will be cut off and die, but a third will be left in the land" (Zechariah 13:8 TLB).

"WATCH, FOR the day of the Lord is coming soon! On that day the Lord will gather together the nations to fight Jerusalem; the city will be taken, the houses rifled, the loot divided, the women raped; half the population will be taken away as slaves, and half will be left in what remains of the city" (Zechariah 14:1-2 TLB).

"Therefore when you see the 'abomination of desolation,' spoken of by Daniel the prophet, standing in the holy place (whoever reads, let him understand), then let those who are in Judea flee to the mountains.

Let him who is on the housetop not come down to take anything out of his house.

And let him who is in the field not go back to get his clothes.

But woe to those who are pregnant and to those with nursing babies in those days!

And pray that your flight may not be in winter or on the Sabbath.

For then there will be great tribulation, such as has not been since the beginning of the world until this time, no, nor ever shall be.

And unless those days were shortened, no flesh would be saved; but for the elect's sake those days will be shortened" (Matthew 24:14-22 NKJ).

". . .These are the ones coming out of the Great Tribulation. . ." (Revelation 7:14 TLB).

Chapter 12—The Jews Will Go Through Tribulation

Study Guide 11

1. State the purpose of the tribulation period.

   Prepare the Jews for The Messiah (Jesus)

2. State what the Antichrist will do that will convince the Jews to sign a peace treaty with him.

   Provide protection. So Jews can build a Temple & perform their ancient religion

3. Explain what will happen that will cause the Antichrist to persecute the Jews.

   Jews will not worship Antichrist as Messiah. They will not like his image placed in the temple

4. State what affect the tribulation period will have on the Jewish people concerning Jesus of Nazareth.

   Many Jews will accept Jesus as Messiah

13

The Jews Will Return To God

As horrible as this tribulation period will be, God will use it to turn the heart of the Jew back to Him. When the Jewish people once again seek God with their whole heart, their spiritual blindness will be removed. They will then recognize Jesus as their Messiah and turn to Him on a national basis.

For the time being, God has been bringing the Jews back to their land in their state of unbelief. The prophet Ezekiel said this would happen when he spoke about the Jews returning to their land with no breath in them (Ezekiel 37:8). By this he meant the Spirit of God.

Orthodox Jews do not recognize and accept the modern restoration of the state of Israel. They believe Scripture teaches that the Messiah will be the one to gather the Jews back to their land (Deuteronomy 30:3-6). This is true.

However, both the present restoration, which is political, and the orthodox view, which is religious, are scriptural. God is bringing the Jews back to their land in unbelief as Ezekiel predicted. But as we've just learned, the Antichrist will scatter them for a short time (Zechariah 14:1-2). It is at this time that Messiah Jesus will come and regather them back to the land. Jesus spoke of this final regathering and said that He was the one who would come and defeat the Antichrist, then lead the scattered Jews back to their land (Matthew 24:29-31).

God's Providence Revealed

As we read about what is taking place in Israel today, we discover that even now the Jews are beginning to experience a renewed awareness of God's protection over them. As of this writing, the Jews have fought four wars since becoming an independent nation. They have also been involved in the crisis in Lebanon.

In all of these wars, the Jews have been completely outnumbered by their hostile Arab neighbors whose stated intention is to destroy them all. Yet against enemies that it seemed could easily overwhelm them, the Jews have won each war. How can this be? There's only one answer. God is miraculously interceding on their behalf, and the Jews are beginning to figure that out.

God's providential care will become even more clear to the Jews when He defeats Russia. It is inconceivable to think that the little nation of Israel could win a war against Russia. Humanly speaking, it is impossible. But with God all things are possible. God overrides man's evil and uses it for His glory and the good of those He has called to be His own. In this instance, He destroys the Russian army with the result being the Jews will realize it was God who saved them. The whole world will also realize it.

Ezekiel wrote:

"Thus will I show my greatness and bring honor upon my name, and all the nations of the world will hear

122

what I have done, and know that I am God" (Ezekiel 38:23 TLB)!

"Thus I will make known my holy name among my people Israel; I will not let it be mocked anymore. And the nations too shall know I am the Lord, the Holy One of Israel" (Ezekiel 39:7 TLB).

"Thus I will demonstrate my glory among the nations; all shall see the punishment of Gog (Russia) and know that I have done it" (Ezekiel 39:21 TLB).

"And from that time onward, the people of Israel will know I am the Lord their God" (Ezekiel 39:22 TLB).

The Anger Of The Nations

However, there will be no letup of pressure against Israel. The nations of the world will still hate the Jewish people. *Through satanic power to perform miracles, the Antichrist will persuade the nations to move their military armament into the Middle East to finish off the Jews and defeat their coming Messiah. This will be the final "final solution" to the Jewish problem and will take place at the very end of the tribulation period.*

The following Scriptures tell us that all nations will come against Israel at this point:

"For they are the spirits of devils, working miracles, which go forth unto the kings of the earth and of the whole world, to gather them to the battle of that great day of God Almighty" (Revelation 16:14 KJV).

"I will gather the armies of the world into the 'Valley Where Jehovah Judges' and punish them there for harming my people, for scattering my inheritance among the nations and dividing up my land" (Joel 3:2 TLB).

"I see full well what they are doing; I know what they are thinking, so I will gather together all nations and people against Jerusalem, where they shall see my glory" (Isaiah 66:18 TLB).

"THIS IS the fate of Israel, as pronounced by the Lord, who stretched out the heavens and laid the foundation of the earth, and formed the spirit of man within him:

I will make Jerusalem and Judah like a cup of poison to all the nearby nations that send their armies to surround Jerusalem. Jerusalem will be a heavy stone burdening the world. And though all the nations of the earth unite in an attempt to move her, they will all be crushed.

'In that day,' says the Lord, 'I will bewilder the armies drawn up against her, and make fools of them, for I will watch over the people of Judah, but blind all her enemies.

And the clans of Judah shall say to themselves, 'The people of Jerusalem have found strength in the Lord of Hosts, their God.'

"The Lord will defend the people of Jerusalem; the weakest among them will be as mighty as King David! And the royal line will be as God, like the Angel of the Lord who goes before them! For my plan is to destroy all the nations that come against Jerusalem" (Zechariah 12:1-5, 8-9 TLB).

"For I will gather all nations against Jerusalem to battle. . ." (Zechariah 14:2 KJV).

The Last Great Battle
    This is the great battle of Armageddon to which the whole world is heading. John wrote in Revelation 16:16, "And he gathered them together into a place called in the Hebrew tongue Armageddon" (KJV).
    Armageddon is the name of a mountain in Israel. At the foot of the mountain is the valley of Megiddo. This valley is about ten miles south of Nazareth and about fifteen miles from the Mediterranean. This valley has been the scene of more battles than any other spot on planet earth. But this one will be the bloodiest of them all. The battlefield will be

200 miles long and one hundred miles wide. *Jerusalem is right in the middle.*

We get a picture of this battle in the following Scriptures:

"WHAT FOOLS the nations are to rage against the Lord! How strange that men should try to outwit God! For a summit conference of the nations has been called to plot against the Lord and his Messiah, Christ, the King. 'Come, let us break his chains, they say, and free ourselves from all this slavery to God.'

But God in heaven merely laughs! He is amused by all their puny plans. And then in fierce fury he rebukes them and fills them with fear.

For the Lord declares, "This is the King of my choice, and I have enthroned him in Jerusalem, my holy city" (Psalm 2:1-6 TLB).

"COME HERE and listen, O nations of the earth; let the world and everything in it hear my words. For the Lord is enraged against the nations; his fury is against their armies. He will utterly destroy them and deliver them to slaughter. Their dead will be left unburied, and the stench of rotting bodies will fill the land, and the mountains will flow with their blood" (Isaiah 34:1-3 TLB).

"I have trodden the winepress alone. No one was there to help me. In my wrath I have trodden my enemies like grapes. In my fury I trampled my foes. It is their blood you see upon my clothes. For the time has come for me to avenge my people, to redeem them from the hands of their oppressors. I looked but no one came to help them; I was amazed and appalled. So I executed vengenance alone; unaided, I meted out judgement. I crushed the heathen nations in my anger and made them stagger and fall to the ground" (Isaiah 63:3-6 TLB).

"OH, THAT you would burst forth from the skies and come down! How the mountains would quake in your presence! The consuming fire of your glory would burn down the forests and boil the oceans dry. The nations would tremble before you; then your enemies would learn the reason for your fame" (Isaiah 64:1-2 TLB)!

" 'AT THAT time, when I restore the prosperity of Judah and Jerusalem,' says the Lord, 'I will gather the armies of the world into the 'Valley Where Jehovah Judges' and punish them there for harming my people, for scattering my inheritance among the nations and dividing up my land'" (Joel 3:1-2 TLB).

"Announce this far and wide: Get ready for war! Conscript your best soldiers; collect all your armies. Melt your plowshares into swords and beat your pruning hooks into spears. Let the weak be strong. Gather together and come, all nations everywhere.

And now, O Lord, bring down your warriors! Collect the nations; bring them to the Valley of Jehoshaphat, for there I will sit to pronounce judgement on them all. Now let the sickle do its work; the harvest is ripe and waiting. Tread the winepress, for it is full to overflowing with the wickedness of these men.

Multitudes, multitudes waiting in the valley for the verdict of their doom! For the Day of The Lord is near, in the Valley of Judgement.

The sun and moon will be darkened and the stars withdraw their light. The Lord shouts from his temple in Jerusalem and the earth and sky begin to shake. But to his people Israel, the Lord will be very gentle. He is their Refuge and Strength. 'Then you shall know at last that I am the Lord your God in Zion, my holy mountain. Jerusalem shall be mine forever; the time will come when no foreign armies will pass through her any more'" (Joel 3:9-17 TLB).

"Be patient; the time is coming soon when I will stand up and accuse these evil nations. For it is my decision to gather together the kingdoms of the earth, and pour out my fiercest anger and wrath upon them. All the earth shall be devoured with the fire of my jealousy.

Sing, O daughter of Zion; shout, O Israel; be glad and rejoice with all your heart, O daughter of Jerusalem. For the Lord will remove his hand of judgement, and disperse the armies of your enemy. And the Lord himself, the King of Israel, will live among you! At last your troubles will be over—you need fear no more" (Zephaniah 3:8,14-15 TLB).

"I will make Jerusalem and Judah like a cup of poison to all the nearby nations that send their armies to surround Jerusalem. Jerusalem will be a heavy stone burdening the world. And though all the nations of the earth unite in an attempt to move her, they will all be crushed."

"In that day, says the Lord, I will bewilder the armies drawn up against her, and make fools of them, for I will watch over the people of Judah, but blind all her enemies.

The Lord will defend the people of Jerusalem; the weakest among them will be as mighty as King David! And the royal line will be as God, like the Angel of the Lord who goes before them! For my plan is to destroy all the nations that come against Jerusalem" (Zechariah 12:2-4,8-9 TLB).

"WATCH, FOR the day of the Lord is coming soon! On that day the Lord will gather together the nations to fight Jerusalem; the city will be taken, the houses rifled, the loot divided, the women raped; half the population will be taken away as slaves, and half will be left in what remains of the city.

Then the Lord will go out fully armed for war, to fight against those nations. That day his feet will stand upon the Mount of Olives, to the east of Jerusalem, and the Mount of Olives will split apart, making a very wide valley running from east to west, for half the mountain will move toward the north and half toward the south. You will escape through that valley, for it will reach across to the city gate. . .

"And the Lord will send a plague on all the people who fought Jerusalem. They will become like walking corpses, their flesh rotting away; their eyes will shrivel in their sockets, and their tongues will decay in their mouths. They will be seized with terror, panic-stricken from the Lord, and will fight against each other in hand-to-hand combat. All Judah will be fighting at Jerusalem. The wealth of all the neighboring nations will be confiscated. . ." (Zechariah 14:1-5,12-14 TLB).

"Then the scene changed and I saw a white cloud and someone sitting on it who looked like Jesus, who was called 'The Son of Man,' with a crown of solid gold upon his head and a sharp sickle in his hand.

Then an angel came from the temple and called out to him, 'Begin to use the sickle, for the time has come for you to reap; the harvest is ripe on the earth.' So the one sitting on the cloud swung his sickle over the earth, and the harvest was gathered in. After that another angel came from the temple in heaven, and he also had a sharp sickle.

Just then the angel who has power to destroy the world with fire, shouted to the angel with the sickle, Use your sickle now to cut off the clusters of grapes from the vines of the earth, for they are fully ripe for judgement.' So the angel swung his sickle on the earth and loaded the grapes into the great winepress of God's wrath. And the grapes were trodden in the winepress outside the city, and blood flowed in a stream 200 miles long and as high as a horse's bridle" (Revelation 14:14-20 TLB).

The Coming Of The Messiah

The preaching of the 144,000 evangelists and the ministry of the two prophets will have led many Jews to acknowledge and receive Jesus as their Messiah. *As they realize the Antichrist and the Gentile nations are about to totally destroy them, this godly remnant of Jewish believers will call upon Jesus to come and deliver them.* God will not disappoint them. He responds by giving Jesus the signal to return to planet earth as the lion of the tribe of Judah who will rescue the Jewish believers and establish the throne of David and God in Jerusalem.

John describes the return of Messiah Jesus and His victory over the Antichrist in these words:

"Then I saw heaven opened and a white horse standing there; and the one sitting on the horse was named 'Faithful and true'—the one who justly punishes and makes war. His eyes were like flames, and on his head were many crowns. A name was written on his forehead, and only he knows its meaning. He was clothed with garments dipped in blood, and his title was 'The Word of God.' The armies of heaven, dressed in finest linen, white and clean, followed him on white horses.

In his mouth he held a sharp sword to strike down the nations; he ruled them with an iron grip; and he trod the winepress of the fierceness of the wrath of Almighty God. On his robe and thigh was written this title: 'King of Kings and Lord of Lords' "(Revelation 19:11-16 TLB).

"Then I saw an angel standing in the sunshine, shouting loudly to the birds, 'Come! Gather together for the supper of the great God! Come and eat the flesh of kings, and captains, and great generals; of horses and riders; and of all humanity, both great and small, slave and free' " (Revelation 19:17-18 TLB).

"Then I saw the Evil Creature (Antichrist) gathering the governments of the earth and their armies to fight against the one sitting on the horse and his army. And the Evil Creature was captured, and with him the False Prophet, who could do mighty miracles when the Evil

Creature was present—miracles that deceived all who had accepted the Evil Creature's mark, and who worshiped his statue. Both of them—the Evil Creature and his False Prophet—were thrown alive into the Lake of Fire that burns with sulphur. And their entire army was killed with the sharp sword in the mouth of the one riding the white horse, and all the birds of heaven were gorged with their flesh" (Revelation 19:19-21 TLB).

Scripture References

Here are some Scriptures that tell us a remnant of the Jews will return to God and by doing so will accept Jesus as their Messiah:

"And the Lord your God will circumcise your heart and the heart of your descendants, to love the Lord your God with all your heart and with all your soul, that you may live" (Deuteronomy 30:6 NKJ).

"Then I will give them a heart to know Me, that I am the Lord; and they shall be My people, and I will be their God, for they shall return to Me with their whole heart" (Jeremiah 24:7 NKJ).

"And I will give them one heart and mind to worship me forever, for their own good and the good of all their descendants. And I will make an everlasting covenant with them, promising never again to desert them, but only to do them good. I will put a desire in their hearts to worship me, and they shall never leave me" (Jeremiah 32:39-40 TLB).

"I will give you one heart and a new spirit; I will take from you your hearts of stone and give you tender hearts of love for God, so that you can obey my laws and be my people, and I will be your God" (Ezekiel 11:19-20 TLB).

"And I will give you a new heart—I will give you new and right desires—and put a new spirit within you. I will take out your stony hearts of sin and give you new hearts of love. And I will put my spirit within you so that you will obey my laws and do whatever I command.

"And you shall live in Israel, the land which I gave your fathers long ago. And you shall be my people and I will be your God" (Ezekiel 36:26-28 TLB).

"This illustrates the fact that Israel will be a long time without a king or prince, and without an altar, temple, priests, or even idols!

Afterward they will return to the Lord their God, and to the Messiah, their King, and they shall come trembling, submissive to the Lord and to his blessings, in the end times" (Hosea 3:4-5 TLB).

"And I will pour on the house of David and on the inhabitants of Jerusalem the Spirit of grace and supplication; then they will look upon Me whom they have pierced; they will mourn for Him as one mourns for his only son, and grieve for Him as one grieves for a firstborn" (Zechariah 12:10 NKJ).

"In that day a fountain shall be opened for the house of David and for the inhabitants of Jerusalem, for sin and for uncleanness.

I will bring the one-third through the fire, Will refine them as silver is refined, And test them as gold is tested. They will call on My name, And I will answer them. I will say, 'This is My people'; And each one will say, 'The Lord is my God' " (Zechariah 13:1,9 NKJ).

"O Jerusalem, Jerusalem, the one who kills the prophets and stones those who are sent to her! How often I wanted to gather your children together, as a hen gathers her chicks under her wings, but you were not willing!

"See! Your house is left to you desolate; for I say to you, you shall see Me no more till you say, 'Blessed is He who comes in the name of the Lord' " (Matthew 23;37-39 NKJ)!

Chapter 13—The Jews Will Return To God

Study Guide 12

1. State what affect God's destruction of Russia will have on the nations of the world, including Israel.

   They all will realize that God had saved them

2. Explain why all nations will eventually fight against Israel.

   The antichrist will persuade them.

3. State how the Battle of Armageddon ends in relationship to the nation of Israel.

   The lord will destroy all those who come against her with the sword from his mouth. The lord will change the hearts of the Isrealites.

14

God Will Remember His Covenant

We now come to the last of Moses' ten-point prediction. As we've learned in the previous chapters, God's covenant with Abraham was the most sacred of all compacts. It was a literal, unconditional, everlasting covenant that absolutely cannot be broken. And although any one generation of Hebrews could dishonor the covenant, the covenant itself remained in force.

The three particular covenant blessings God promised Abraham and his descendants were a land, a nation and spiritual blessings through the Messiah. These blessings were conditional based on the Hebrews' obedience to God. Tragically, the Hebrews were not obedient. They worshiped other gods in spite of God's continuous warnings from the prophets. As a result, the Jews were driven from their land,

135

banished as a nation and missed the blessings offered to them by Messiah Jesus.

Yet God has not forgotten His covenant people. He has preserved a remnant throughout history and brought them back to the land where He is going to make them a great nation and turn their hearts back to Him. Then, as we've seen, Jesus will come and rule, not only as King of the Jews, but as King of kings and Lord of lords.

When Messiah Jesus returns, He will rule planet earth from Jerusalem (Isaiah 2:2-4). Israel will be the head nation of the world (Deuteronomy 28:13; Zechariah 8:23). They will live in peace among their neighbors in the land God promised them (Isaiah 2:4). The blessings of Messiah Jesus will be enjoyed by all. *It is at this time that God's three covenant promises to Abraham will find their complete fulfillment.* Let's now take a closer look at this golden age that lies ahead for the Jewish people and all who await the coming of Jesus.

The Messianic Kingdom

This golden age is called the Messianic kingdom because it is the period of time when God will rule planet earth through Messiah Jesus. We learn in the Hebrew Scriptures that it was God's desire to rule Israel as their king (1 Samuel 8:9). But the Jews wanted a human king like the nations among them (1 Samuel 8:5). God granted their request and gave them human kings. But none of these kings could rule with the perfect moral character of God. Being only human, they failed in many ways. In view of this, God determined that He would rule them Himself through the person of Messiah Jesus.

The Bible says this Messianic kingdom will last for 1,000 years (Revelation 20:1-7). This period of time is known as the Millennium, from the Latin words milli (one thousand) and annum (year). It's the utopia for which man has so desperately strived, but never achieved. Man has never achieved it because he's tried to achieve it without God.

The Kingdom Of God

One of the main subjects in the Bible is the *"kingdom of God."* The Hebrew prophets often spoke about it (Daniel 7:13-14). In the New Testament Scriptures, John the Baptist preached that the "kingdom is at hand" (Matthew 3:2). Jesus preached the same message (Matthew 4:17). He then sent out His disciples to preach the kingdom of God (Matthew 10:7).

When we speak of a kingdom, we think of a king, a people and a territory over which the king rules. *When the Bible speaks of the kingdom of God, it means the rule of God through Messiah Jesus over a people and a territory.*

There are two realms of the kingdom of God. One is spiritual and the other is physical. One day the religious leaders asked Jesus some questions about the kingdom. Jesus replied that the kingdom of God would be within a person (Luke 17:21). The apostle Paul wrote: "for the kingdom of God is not food and drink, but righteousness and peace and joy in the Holy Spirit" (Romans 14:17 NKJ). Jesus rules as king in the hearts of all who have received Him as their personal Messiah and Lord. That rule is manifested as one lives under the control of God's Holy Spirit.

Jesus offered a physical kingdom to the Jews as well as a spiritual one. They didn't like the kind of offer He made, so they rejected Him as their king. They said ". . . We have no king but Caesar" (John 19:15 KJV). By rejecting Jesus as their Messiah, the Jews were showing that they still rejected God's rule over them. Jesus then offered the spiritual aspects of the kingdom of God to the Gentiles. Today, every individual Jew and Gentile who accepts His offer becomes part of a new company of people—called the church. The church presently lives in the spiritual realm of the kingdom of God.

When God completes His time of forming the church, which He calls the fullness of the Gentiles (Romans 11:25), He will once again offer a physical, literal kingdom to the Jews as a nation. At this time, as we've just learned, the

Jews will be prepared to accept God's offer and acknowledge Jesus as their king. This is the Messianic kingdom.

When Jesus returns, there will be certain divine judgements on those who have survived the tribulation period (Ezekiel 20:34-38; Matthew 25:31-46). This is to determine who will be able to enter into the Messianic kingdom in their earthly bodies. The result of this judgement is that only believing Jews and Gentiles will enter the kingdom. The rest will be cut off and banished from His presence.

The Messianic Government

The type of government during the Messianic kingdom will be a *theocracy*. This means that God Himself will rule as king over all the earth through Messiah Jesus. This theocracy will unite in Messiah Jesus, both the kingdom of God and the kingdom of David. Jesus, as the divine Son of God, will administer the kingdom of God through the resurrected believers of all ages. Jesus, as the human Son of David, will administer the kingdom of David through the remnant of believing Jews who are alive at His coming, and who will enter into the Messianic kingdom.

Thus all believers shall rule with Jesus. Resurrected believers will have a part in the administration of the kingdom of God. This will involve the heavenly aspects of the kingdom on earth. The Jewish believers will have their part in the administration of the kingdom of David. This will involve the earthly aspects of the kingdom (Daniel 7:18,22,27; Romans 8:17).

The blessings of the kingdom of God will come to the Gentiles through the nation of Israel as they live under the righteous rule of Messiah Jesus who will sit on the throne of David (Isaiah 49:6; 62:2; 11:10; Jeremiah 3:17; 16:19-21).

The writer of Psalm 2 gives us a clear statement concerning the rule of Jesus in the Messianic kingdom. He writes:

"For the Lord God declares, 'This is the King of my choice, and I have enthroned him in Jerusalem, my holy city.'

His chosen one replies, 'I will reveal the everlasting purposes of God, for the Lord has said to me, 'You are my Son. This is your coronation day. Today I am giving you your glory.' Only ask, and I will give you all the nations of the world. Rule them with an iron rod; smash them like clay pots' " (Psalm 2:6-9 TLB)!

Daniel was privileged to have a vision of the coming of Messiah Jesus in all of His glory and power to rule as king. Daniel wrote:

"During the reigns of those kings, the God of heaven will set up a kingdom that will never be destroyed; no one will ever conquer it. It will shatter all these kingdoms into nothingness, but it shall stand forever, indestructible" (Daniel 2:44 TLB).

"Next I saw the arrival of a Man—or so he seemed to be—brought there on clouds from heaven; he approached the Ancient of Days and was presented to him. He was given the ruling power and glory over all the nations of the world, so that all people of every language must obey him. His power is eternal—it will never end; his government shall never fall" (Daniel 7;13-14 TLB).

The prophet Isaiah often spoke about the kingdom of God. One of his more well-known statements reads like this in the Living Bible:

"For unto us a child is born; unto us a Son is given; and the government shall be upon his shoulder. These will be his royal titles: 'Wonderful,' 'Counselor,' 'The Mighty God,' 'The Everlasting Father,' 'The Prince of Peace.' His ever-expanding, peaceful government will never end. He will rule with perfect fairness and justice from the throne of his father David. He will bring true justice and peace to all the nations of the world. This is going to happen because the Lord of heaven's armies has dedicated himself to do it" (Isaiah 9:6-7 TLB).

139

Jerusalem—the World Capital

Jesus will rule from Jerusalem which will be the capital of the world. The news media and wire services will dateline their stories from Jerusalem, not Washington, Moscow, Paris or London. The nations of the world will submit to the policies that the Messiah decrees from the holy city of God. The ancient prophets spoke of this time when Jerusalem would be the center of the world government.

Isaiah prophecied: "In the last days Jerusalem and the Temple of the Lord will become the world's greatest attraction, and people from many lands will flow there to worship the Lord. 'Come,' everyone will say, 'Let us go up the mountain of the Lord, to the Temple of the God of Israel; there he will teach us his laws, and we will obey them.' For in those days the world will be ruled from Jerusalem" (Isaiah 2:2-3 TLB).

Isaiah also declared: "In that day he who created the royal dynasty of David will be a banner of salvation to all the world. The nations will rally to him, for the land where he lives will be a glorious place" (Isaiah 11:10 TLB).

Jeremiah said: "For the Lord himself will be among you, and the whole city of Jerusalem will be known as the throne of the Lord, and all nations will come to him there and no longer stubbornly follow their evil desires" (Jeremiah 3:17 TLB).

Micah wrote: "BUT IN the last days Mount Zion will be the most renowned of all the mountains of the world, praised by all nations; people from all the world will make pilgrimages there. 'Come,' they will say to one another, 'let us visit the mountain of the Lord, and see the Temple of the God of Israel; he will tell us what to do, and we will do it.' For in those days the whole world will be ruled by the Lord from Jerusalem! He will issue his laws and announce his decrees from there" (Micah 4:1-2 TLB).

Zechariah predicted: "In the end, those who survive the plague will go up to Jerusalem each year to worship the King, the Lord of Hosts, to celebrate a time of thanksgiving" (Zechariah 14:16 TLB).

Jesus warned people not to swear by Jerusalem for "It is the city of the great king" (Matthew 5:35).

A Unified Government

The Messianic kingdom will be the true and lasting one-world government that the nations are now trying to establish, but without God. There will be no need for a United Nations. *Jesus will rule with absolute authority and power. All nations will submit to Him, and no open rebellion will be tolerated.* In addition to the Scriptures just noted, the following references give us further insight:

"Only ask, and I will give you all the nations of the world. Rule them with an iron rod; smash them like clay pots" (Psalm 2:8-9 TLB).

"JEHOVAH SAID to my Lord the Messiah, 'Rule as my regent—I will subdue your enemies and make them bow low before you.

Jehovah has established your throne in Jerusalem to rule over your enemies" (Psalm 110:1-2 TLB).

". . .He shall strike the earth with the rod of His mouth, And with the breath of His lips He shall slay the wicked" (Isaiah 11:4 NKJ).

"And the Lord shall be King over all the earth. In that day there shall be one Lord—his name alone will be worshiped" (Zechariah 14:9 TLB).

"In his mouth he held a sharp sword to strike down the nations; he ruled them with an iron grip; and he trod the winepress of the fierceness of the wrath of Almighty God. On his robe and thigh was written this title: 'King of Kings and Lord of Lords' " (Revelation 19:15-16 TLB).

". . .The kingdom of this world now belongs to our

Lord, and to his Christ; and he shall reign forever and ever" (Revelation 11:15 TLB).

A Righteous Rule

Jesus will rule with righteousness and justice for all. All social problems will be solved. No one will be oppressed, taken advantage of, or cheated in any way. There will be no social workers, discrimination, inequities or inequalities of any kind. The Hebrew Scriptures declare:

"But the Lord lives on forever; he sits upon his throne to judge justly the nations of the world. All who are oppressed may come to him. He is a refuge for them in their times of trouble" (Psalm 9:7-9 TLB).

"He will not judge by appearance, false evidence, or hearsay, but will defend the poor and the exploited. He will rule against the wicked who oppress them. For he will be clothed with fairness and with truth" (Isaiah 11:3-5 TLB).

". . .God will establish David's throne forever, and on that throne he will place a just and righteous king" (Isaiah 16:5 TLB).

"For the time is coming, says the Lord, when I will place a righteous Branch upon King David's throne. He shall be a King who shall rule with wisdom and justice and cause righteousness to prevail everywhere throughout the earth. And this is his name: The Lord Our Righteousness. At that time Judah will be saved and Israel will live in peace" (Jeremiah 23:5-6 TLB).

Peace At Last

Because Jesus will be able to rule absolutely with perfect justice and righteousness, *peace will finally come to the earth.* There will no longer be border disputes between neighboring countries. Nations will not seek to dominate others. The military academies will be closed and the war machines dismantled. We learn from the prophets:

"The Lord will settle international disputes; all the nations will convert their weapons of war into implements of peace. Then at last all wars will stop and all military training will end" (Isaiah 2:4 TLB).

"He will arbitrate among the nations, and dictate to strong nations far away. They will beat their swords into plowshares and their spears into pruning-hooks; nations shall no longer fight each other, for all war will end. There will be universal peace, and all the military academies and training camps will be closed down" (Micah 4:3 TLB).

The Messianic Religion

The Messianic kingdom will also have a one-world religion. But it won't be the World Counsel of Churches. Both the political and spiritual aspects of the Messianic kingdom will center in the Messiah. Jesus will rule as the King-Priest uniting both functions in Himself.

Zechariah wrote: ". . . He will rule as both King and as Priest, with perfect harmony between the two" (Zechariah 6:13 TLB).

Because of man's sinful nature, it is not wise for the political and religious affairs of a nation to be under one authority. An ungodly leader who controlled both of these could become a ruthless dictator destroying and corrupting lives in the worst kind of way. This is exactly what the Antichrist will do in the great tribulation.

But Jesus will be able to function in both capacities because He is the perfect God-man. *He will exercise His political authority with perfect righteousness, while keeping the spiritual worship pure and free from perversion.* Jerusalem will not only be the world's capital, it will also be the religious center of the world.

Jeremiah wrote: "But, says the Lord, when I bring you home again from your captivity and restore your fortunes, Jerusalem will be rebuilt upon her ruins; the place will be reconstructed as it was before. The cities will be filled with joy and great thanksgiving, and I will multiply my people and make of them a great and honored nation. Their children shall prosper as in David's reign; their nations shall be established before me, and I will punish anyone who hurts them. They will have their own ruler again. He will not be a foreigner. And I will invite him to be a priest at my altars, and he shall approach me, for who would dare to come unless invited. And you shall be my people and I will be your God" (Jeremiah 30:18-22 TLB).

The prophet Ezekiel provides information concerning worship activities during the Messianic kingdom (Ezekiel 40-48). In these chapters, Ezekiel describes a religious system that includes a temple, priesthood and sacrifices. Although the Messiah will be the center of worship, He will use the religious system as a physical object lesson to show in a tangible way who He is and what He has done. The religious teachers will use these object lessons to point people who are born during the Millennium to the Messiah and their need for Him as personal Lord and Savior.

The presence of the Messiah will insure great spiritual blessings for everyone. *People from all the nations will journey to Jerusalem to worship the King* (Zechariah 14:16). All citizens will be able to have full knowledge of God through the Messiah and will enjoy the new covenant blessings to the fullest (Isaiah 11:9-10).

Messianic Living Conditions

Living conditions in the Messianic kingdom will be blessed beyond our present abilities to imagine. As just noted, there will be *no more wars* (Isaiah 2:4; Micha 4:1-4). In view of this, we won't need to dispatch peace-keeping forces to different trouble spots on the globe. There will be no iron curtain, Berlin wall, demilitarized zones, revolutions, or terrorist groups. The vast sums of money which are now spent on the arms race will be used for the benefit of mankind.

Because Jesus will rule with perfect justice and righteousness, *social problems will no longer burden society.* Everyone will have an equal opportunity to work and provide for their family with dignity and honor. There will be a fair day's wage for a fair day's work. The rich will not be allowed to exploit the poor. There will be no special interest groups in Jerusalem seeking to gain favor at the expense of others. Messianic justice will be administered to all citizens without partiality.

There will be great economic prosperity and full employment (Isaiah 65:21-23; Joel 2:24-26). Government housing, welfare and ghettos will be a thing of the past. There will be no need for food relief programs. Everyone will have plenty to eat for the earth will be greatly productive (Amos 9:13-14).

Management and labor will work together for the common good. There will be no need for collective bargaining or crippling strikes that cut off needed services and goods. Plants will operate at full capacity. The world's economy will stabilize without the ups and downs of inflation and depression. Goods and services will be freely exchanged for the benefit of all.

Moral conditions will conform to the biblical standard (Isaiah 2:3). We won't need the Moral Majority to raise our moral consciousness, nor the Coalition for Better Television to rate the networks. There will be no smut peddlers, drug pushers, drunk drivers, pimps, prostitutes, gambling halls, crime or violence of any kind allowed.

The curse of sin will be partially removed (Romans 8:19-23). The result is that life expectancy will be lengthened so that a 100-year-old person will be considered a child (Isaiah 65:20). There will be no use for hospitals as there will be little or no sickness and death (Isaiah 33:24; Jeremiah 30:17). The world will experience a great population explosion to replenish the earth (Jeremiah 30:19-20). To make communication easier, everyone will speak the same language—Hebrew (Zephaniah 3:9). Light will be increased seven-fold so that more can be accomplished (Zechariah 14:6-7). The land will be fruitful (Isaiah 35:1-2; Zechariah

8:12). Even the animals will live together in peace (Isaiah 11:6-9; 65:25). In every way, life will be better than we can possibly imagine because God will remember His covenant with Abraham.

Scripture References

Some Scriptures that remind us God will remember His covenant are as follows:

"But at last they shall confess their sins and their fathers' sins of treachery against me. (Because they were against me, I was against them, and brought them into the land of their enemies.) When at last their evil hearts are humbled and they accept the punishment I send them for their sins, then I will remember again my promises (covenant) with Abraham, Isaac, and Jacob, and I will remember the land (and its desolation). For the land shall enjoy its Sabbaths as it lies desolate. But then at last they shall accept my punishment for rejecting my laws and for despising my rule. But despite all they have done, I will not utterly destroy them and my covenant with them, for I am Jehovah their God. . ." (Leviticus 26:40-45 TLB).

"But Zion said, The LORD has forsaken me, And my LORD has forgotten me.

Can a woman forget her nursing child, And not have compassion on the son of her womb? Surely they may forget. Yet I will not forget you" (Isaiah 49:14-15 NKJ).

"Behold, the days are coming, says the Lord, when I will make a new covenant with the house of Israel and with the house of Judah-

not according to the covenant that I made with their fathers in the day that I took them by the hand to bring them out of the land of Egypt, My covenant which they broke, though I was a husband to them, says the Lord.

But this is the covenant that I will make with the house of Israel: After those days, says the Lord, I will put My

146

laws in their minds, and write it on their hearts; and I will be their God, and they shall be My people.

No more shall every man teach his neighbor, and every man his brother, saying, 'Know the Lord,' for they shall all know Me, from the least of them to the greatest of them, says the Lord. For I will forgive their iniquity, and their sin I will remember no more" (Jeremiah 31:31-34 NKJ).

"Nevertheless the time will come when I will heal Jerusalem's damage and give her prosperity and peace. I will rebuild the cities of both Judah and Israel and restore their fortunes. And I will cleanse away all their sins against me, and pardon them" (Jeremiah 31:6-8 TLB).

"Have you heard what people are saying?—that the Lord chose Judah and Israel and then abandoned them! They are sneering and saying that Israel isn't worthy to be counted as a nation. But this is the Lord's reply: I would no more reject my people than I would change my laws of night and day, of earth and sky. I will never abandon the Jews, or David my servant, or change the plan that his Child will someday rule these descendants of Abraham, Isaac and Jacob. Instead I will restore their prosperity and have mercy on them" (Jeremiah 33:24-26 TLB).

"I will bring Israel home again to her own land . . . In those days, says the Lord, no sin shall be found in Israel or in Judah, for I will pardon the remnant I preserve" (Jeremiah 50:19-20 TLB).

"I will reaffirm my covenant with you, and you will know I am the Lord. Despite all you have done, I will be kind to you again; you will cover your mouth in silence and in shame when I forgive you all that you have done, says the Lord God" (Ezekiel 16:62-63 TLB).

"I will bring them home from the lands of their enemies—and my glory shall be evident to all the nations when I do it. Through them I will vindicate my holiness before the nations. Then my people will know I am the Lord their God—responsible for sending them away to exile, and responsible for bringing them home. I will leave none of them remaining among the nations. And I will never hide my face from them again, for I will pour out my Spirit upon them, says the Lord God" (Ezekiel 39:27-29 TLB).

"I want you to know about this truth from God, dear brothers, so that you (Gentiles) will not feel proud and start bragging. Yes, it is true that some of the Jews have set themselves against the Gospel now, but this will last only until all of you Gentiles have come to Christ—those of you who will. And then all Israel will be saved. Do you remember what the prophets said about this? There shall come out of Zion a Deliverer, and he shall turn the Jews from all ungodliness. At that time I will take away their sins, just as I promised.

Now many of the Jews are enemies of the Gospel. They hate it. But this has been a benefit to you, for it has resulted in God's giving his gifts to you Gentiles. Yet the Jews are still beloved of God because of his promises to Abraham, Isaac, and Jacob. For God's gifts and his call can never be withdrawn; he will never go back on his promises" (Romans 11:25-29 TLB).

Chapter 14—God Will Remember His Covenant

Study Guide 13

1. Explain the two realms of the kingdom of God.

   Physical - Jews
   Spiritual - Gentiles

2. Describe the type of government that will exist during the Messianic kingdom.

   Theocracy   God - Jesus - Servants

3. Describe the type of religion that will exist during the Messianic kingdom.

   One world Messianic
   Church + State will not be seperat

4. Describe the living conditions that will exist during the Messianic kingdom.

   Unimaginable. Everything will be ok

15

Why Christians Should Love Jews

For the past 2,000 years, the Jews have been walking (often running) on a trail of tears. The persecution they have experienced at the hands of the Gentiles is horrifying. And although we live in an enlightened age, anti-Jewish feelings still lie dormant waiting for the right moment and conditions to wake them from their slumber. Reports from around the world, particularly Europe, indicate that even now anti-Semitism is raising its ugly head in preparation to vent its wrath against the Jews. The time of Jacob's trouble is near.

As we've looked back into the history of the Jews, we've seen very clearly that Christians have not taken a strong enough stand against this hate and violence directed towards the Jewish people. Neither have we shown them the love which Jesus said was the distinguishing mark of His followers.

True Christians are the only real allies that the Jews have today. The Jewish people do not realize this because they do not understand the difference between the various Gentile religions and true Christianity. Thanks to such organizations as the Christian Embassy in Israel, and others, the Jewish people are beginning to recognize this difference.

Christian support for Israel and the Jewish people does not mean we have to agree with everything they do and not speak out when we feel they are wrong. But we must show them genuine love. You may think this a strange statement, but Christians and Jews need each other. This will become clearer in the future. For this reason, we need to be reminded as to why Christians should love Jews. Although there are many reasons, I have chosen to briefly point out five of them.

1. We Owe Them A Debt

Christians should love the Jewish people because we owe them a debt. On one occasion the apostle Paul took up a collection from the Gentile churches for the Jewish Christians in Jerusalem. He spoke of our debt to them with these words, ". . . I must go down to Jerusalem to take a gift to the Jewish Christians there. For you see, the Christians in Macedonia and Achaia have taken up an offering for those in Jerusalem who are going through such hard times. They were very glad to do this, for they feel that they owe a real debt to the Jerusalem Christians. Why? Because the news about Christ came to these Gentiles from the Church in Jerusalem. And since they received this wonderful spiritual gift of the Gospel from there, they feel that the least they can do in return is to give some material aid" (Romans 15:25-27 TLB).

A Written Debt

As we learned at the beginning of this book, God chose the Jews as the ethnic people through which He would bring knowledge of Himself and salvation to the world. *The Bible was written by Jews.* They faithfully recorded and preserved this written revelation of God, not only for themselves, but for us Gentiles as well. Everytime a sermon or teaching is presented from the Bible, it is a message from God to us written by the hand of a Jew. The only possible exception might be Luke, who may have been a Gentile (Colossians 4:11-14).

A Moral Debt

When God renewed His covenant with the Jews at Mount Sinai, He gave them certain laws by which to live. These laws were to govern the moral, religious and civil life of the Jewish people. The heart of the moral law was the Ten Commandments. When God gave the Ten Commandments, the moral condition of the world was far from God. Idolatry and immorality were the hallmarks of society. Over the centuries, the Ten Commandments caused the world to realize its sinful condition. The result was that a considerable part of Gentile society began to turn from their idols to the one true God, and *their sense of right and wrong was raised to a higher moral* plain. The awareness of God, and high moral standards made possible by the Ten Commandments, delivered us from the worship of dumb idols made with the hands of men and the wicked and perverted ways of the world.

A Spiritual Debt

The three main features of the religious law were the temple, the priesthood and the sacrifice system. God used each of these to teach the Jews the only true way that man could be reconciled to God.

You see, God never intended the Jews to approach Him by trying to keep the Ten Commandments. He knew they could never keep them. The Commandments were just a mirror for the people to see how holy God is and how sinful they were. So the Ten Commandments were not given for the purpose of saving the Jews. The Ten Commandments

153

cannot offer the necessary blood evidence that the penalty for sin has been paid. God intended the Jews to approach Him the way He had established from the beginning with Adam and Eve—through a blood sacrifice for the forgiveness of sin. The individual Jew was saved from his sins through faith in the blood of the innocent substitutionary sacrifice.

God had in mind that when the Jews heard the Ten Commandments, they would run as fast as they could to the temple, kill a lamb and offer its blood in their place as a substitute sin offering to a holy God.

Therefore God established a temple, a sacrifice system and a priesthood as the way for the Jew to approach Him. The Jew was not to approach God by the Ten Commandments but through the sacrifices administered by the priest at the temple (Psalms 50:5).

The temple was the place where God met and dwelled with His covenant people. The glory of God dwelled in their midst in the temple. The High Priest provided the entire nation with representation before God. Through the sacrifices, the Jews could approach God and have their sins forgiven.

God used these provisions of the religious law as object lessons teaching both Jew and Gentile alike how to be reconciled to Him and have our sins forgiven. By seeing this religious law being acted out, we learn that, even though the Commandments condemn us, God has made a way for us to be brought near to Him. This way is through the blood of the innocent substitutionary sacrifice for the forgiveness of sin.

The New Testament Scriptures tell us that God established this way to approach Him as shadows of the real temple, the real sacrifice and the real High Priest who would come later (Colossians 2:17; Hebrews 10:1). This, of course, was Jesus, the Messiah.

Jesus said, "Don't misunderstand why I have come—it isn't to cancel the laws of Moses and the warnings of the prophets. No I came to fulfill them, and to make them all come true" (Matthew 5:17 TLB). By this Jesus was claiming to be the true dwelling place of God in the flesh, the eternal priest from heaven, and the once and for all perfect sacrifice who would take away our sins through His death on the cross. (See John 1:14; Colossians 2:9; Hebrews 9-10).

We can have personal salvation through faith in the blood of Jesus Christ as the innocent substitutionary sacrifice who died for our sins. The Jews were saved by looking forward to His coming through the religious law that pointed to Him. We are saved today by looking back to the time when He came.

Now that Jesus has come, there is no more need to bring animals to a building to be offered by a priest. He made the ultimate sacrifice for us when He gave His own life. When we come to Him as our Lord and Savior, we receive forgiveness of sin and inherit eternal life. God then writes His laws on the fleshy tablets of our hearts. We become the dwelling place of God by receiving the Holy Spirit. This enables all of us to minister as priests of God, and we give ourselves as a living sacrifice to Him.

The blessings of the Messiah have come to us through the Jewish people. Paul expressed this in the following way to the Christians in Ephesus:

"Never forget that once you were heathen, and that you were called godless and 'unclean' by the Jews. (But their hearts, too, were still unclean, even though they were going through the ceremonies and rituals of the godly, for they circumcised themselves as a sign of godliness.) Remember that in those days you were living utterly apart from Christ; you were enemies of God's children and he had promised you no help. You were lost, without God, without hope.

But now you belong to Christ Jesus, and though you once were far away from God, now you have been brought very near to him because of what Jesus Christ has done for you with his blood.

For Christ himself is our way of peace. He had made peace between us Jews and you Gentiles by making us all one family, breaking down the wall of contempt that used to separate us. By his death he ended the angry resentment between us, caused by the Jewish laws which favored the Jews and excluded the Gentiles, for he died to annul the whole system of Jewish laws. Then he took the two groups that had been opposed to each other and made them parts of himself, thus he fused us together to become one new person, and at last there was peace. As parts of the same body, our anger against each other has disappeared, for both of us have been reconciled to God. And so the feud ended at last at the cross. And he has brought this Good News of peace to you Gentiles who were very far away from him, and to us Jews who were near. Now all of us, whether Jews or Gentiles, may come to God the Father with the Holy Spirit's help because of what Christ has done for us.

Now you are no longer strangers to God and foreigners to heaven, but you are members of God's very own family, citizens of God's country, and you belong in God's household with every other Christian.

What a foundation you stand on now: the apostles and the prophets; and the cornerstone of the building is Jesus Christ himself! We who believe are carefully joined together with Christ as parts of a beautiful, constantly growing temple for God. And you also are joined with him and with each other by the Spirit, and are part of this dwelling place of God" (Ephesians 2:11-22 TLB).

A Civil Debt

The Gentile nations, particularly the west, have also greatly benefited from the civil laws that God gave the Jewish people. Ancient nations rarely had an adequate sense of justice. They even had a lesser concern for mercy. The sacredness of human life and the dignity of man were not recognized. The concept of liberty and justice for all was unheard of in the ancient world.

The civil laws that God gave the Jewish people covered all areas of Jewish life. Many of these pertained to marriage and the family. Marriage is the basic institution that God ordained beginning with Adam and Eve. He gave laws to govern it in order to preserve it and keep it from corruption and dissolution.

There were also laws that dealt with crimes against society. These covered crimes of a moral nature, crimes against individuals or their property and crimes against the state. Property rights were also regulated.

In addition to laws concerning individuals, there were laws pertaining to the operation of the state. These laws dealt with the political, social, economic and military affairs of the Hebrew nation.

The purpose of all of these laws was to reveal the moral character of God and ensure a high degree of peace and order among the Jewish people as a nation. *Subsequently, all nations that have a Judeo-Christian heritage have enjoyed a greater degree of civil stability and liberty than they would have otherwise.*

Western society no longer seems to be governed by these divine laws. It will not survive unless it returns to them. Democracies can only exist when the principles given by God to the Jewish people through their civil laws serve as the core of a nation's legal system. When this is no longer true, the result is always anarchy followed by dictatorship.

To summarize this first point, we owe the Jews a debt because they have given us the Bible, a high sense of morality, personal salvation through Messiah Jesus and civil order and liberty.

2. Abraham Is Our Spiritual Father

A second reason Christians should show love to the Jewish people is because Abraham is our spiritual father. Four times the Bible says that Abraham believed God and was counted as righteous (Genesis 15:6; Romans 4:3; Galatians

157

3:6; James 2:23). The question we need to answer is, "What was it Abraham believed?"

Paul answers this for us in his letter to the Galatian Christians. He says, "Know ye therefore that they which are of faith, the same are the children of Abraham. And the Scripture, foreseeing that God would justify the heathen through faith, preached before the gospel unto Abraham, saying, In thee shall all nations be blessed with faithful Abraham" (Galatians 3:7-9 KJV).

Paul states that God preached the gospel to Abraham. A curious question that comes to our mind is how God could preach the gospel to Abraham when Abraham lived 2,000 years before Jesus was born.

God preached the gospel to Abraham by promising Abraham that one of his descendants would be a blessing to the whole world. This descendant was spoken of as the "promised seed." The promised seed of Abraham was to be the Jewish Messiah who would establish the kingdom of God on planet earth and thereby bring both physical and spiritual blessings to the world.

God preached the gospel of the Messiah to Abraham in shadow form through his son Isaac. If you recall, Isaac was born in a supernatural way. At the time of his birth, Abraham was 100 years old, and Sarah was 90. He was impotent and she was past the age of child bearing. In view of this, Abraham definitely believed in a supernatural birth. He believed that God would miraculously bring him a son. God did, and Abraham called his son, Isaac.

As a means of testing Abraham's sincerity, God instructed Abraham to offer Isaac as a sacrifice. It was common practice for devotees of pagan gods to offer their first-born to their gods. Would Abraham do the same for his God? Abraham would, and Abraham did. He believed God enough to offer his only son as a sacrifice.

God told Abraham to take Isaac to a mountain in a city called Salem, later to be called Jerusalem. This was a three-day journey. For the three-day trip to that mountain top, in Abraham's mind, Isaac was as good as dead.

But Abraham was a man of faith. As we learn from the account given in Genesis 22, we find that Abraham believed that God would provide an innocent substitutionary sacrifice for Isaac or raise him from the dead to be the first-born of many covenant children (Hebrews 11:19).

As we follow this touching story, we learn that Abraham also believed that, in later years, God would provide Himself a substitutionary sacrifice greater than Isaac. And Abraham believed that God's own sacrifice would be offered at the very same place where Isaac was offered.

What then do we see that Abraham believed? What did God teach him through Isaac? Abraham believed that God would give him a descendant who would be a blessing to the whole world. This promised seed was to be the Messiah. He would be born supernaturally. He would be God's only Son given as an innocent substitutionary sacrifice for the sins of the world. He would be sacrificed in the very same place where Isaac was offered (Jerusalem). But He would be raised from the dead on the third day to be the first-born of many covenant children of God.

Doesn't that story sound familiar? It sure does. It's the gospel of Messiah Jesus. He was born supernaturally of a virgin birth as a descendant of Abraham. God so loved the world that He gave His only Son as an innocent substitionary sacrifice for our sins. He was sacrificed at the same place where Isaac had been offered 2,000 years earlier. And after three days and nights, He rose from the dead to be the first-born of many covenant children of God.

This is what Jesus meant when He told the Jewish leaders that Abraham saw His day and was glad (John 8:56).

Today, God asks us to believe the same gospel message of the Messiah that he preached to Abraham in shadow form through Isaac. In view of this, the Bible says that Abraham is the spiritual father of all who believe as he believed (Romans 3-4).

Jesus said that the real children of Abraham do the works of Abraham (John 8:39). He also pointed out that the work of Abraham is that Abraham believed the witness of God to His son (John 6:29; Galatians 3:6-9).

Paul said it this way to the Romans, "For he is not a Jew who is one outwardly, nor is that circumcision which is outward in the flesh; but he is a Jew who is one inwardly, and circumcision is that of the heart, in the Spirit, and not in the letter; whose praise is not from men but from God" (Romans 2:28-29 NKJ).

In these verses, Paul declares that the real Jew is not one who has merely had a circumcision of the flesh, but it is one who has had a circumcision of the heart, be they physical Jews or Gentiles. Some other Scriptures that speak about this same subject are: Deuteronomy 10:16; 30:6; Jeremiah 4:4; 9:25-26; 2 Corinthians 5:17; Philippians 3:3.

Paul then states in his letter to the Galatian Christians that Abraham is the spiritual father of all who share Abraham's faith in the gospel concerning the Messiah. He writes:

"that the blessing of Abraham might come upon the Gentiles in Christ Jesus, that we might receive the promise of the Spirit through faith. . . Now to Abraham and his Seed were the promises made. He does not say, 'And to seeds,' as of many, but as of one, 'And to your Seed,' who is Christ. . . But the Scripture has confined all under sin, that the promise by faith in Jesus Christ might be given to those who believe.

For you are all sons of God through faith in Jesus Christ. . .there is neither Jew nor Greek, there is neither slave nor free, there is neither male nor female; for you are all one in Christ Jesus. And if you are Christ's, then you are Abraham's seed, and heirs according to the promise" (Galatians 3:14,16,22,26,28-29 NKJ).

3. God Loves the Jews

A third reason we should love the Jewish people is because God loves them.

We read in the book of Deuteronomy, "The LORD did not set His love on you nor choose you because you were more in number than any other people, for you were the least of all peoples; but because the LORD loves you. . ." (Deuteronomy 7:7-8 NKJ).

The Bible tells us that God is love (1 John 4:8,16). This is perhaps the greatest revelation God has given to us about Himself.

God's love is different from human love in four ways. First of all, it is *holy*. It is not a good-natured sentimentalism that is indifferent to sin. God told the Jews that He loved them. But He also told them they had to put away their idols and immorality or they would forfeit the blessings of the covenant. The Jews would not obey. God had no other choice but to drive them from their land. This discipline from God did not mean that He no longer loved them. It was simply His holy love in action.

King Solomon recognized the holy nature of God's love and wrote, "For whom the LORD loves He corrects" (Proverbs 3:12 NKJ).

God's love is also *eternal*. This means it transcends time. God was love, is love and will be love. He loved the Jews in the past, He loves the Jews now and He will love the Jews in the future.

We've already pointed out that the Jews are a miracle people. They should have vanished from the face of the earth centuries ago. But they are still with us and are stronger now as a people than they have been for 2,500 years. The only possible answer to this incredible survival of the Jewish people is the faithfulness of God to His covenant and His everlasting love.

The prophet Jeremiah predicted that God would preserve the Jews through history and bring them back to their land. He said that God would do this because of His everlasting love. Here are his words:

> "AT THAT time, says the Lord, all the families of Israel shall recognize me as their Lord; they shall act like my

people. I will care for them as I did those who escaped from Egypt, to whom I showed my mercies in the wilderness, when Israel sought for rest. For long ago the Lord had said to Israel: I have loved you, O my people, with an everlasting love; with loving-kindness I have drawn you to me. I will rebuild your nation, O virgin of Israel. You will again be happy and dance merrily with the timbrels. Again you will plant your vineyards upon the mountains of Samaria and eat from your own gardens there" (Jeremiah 31:1-5 TLB).

Jeremiah personally experienced great sorrow and tribulation. Yet he knew that God had not forsaken him and would eventually honor him. He was not only speaking for himself but the Jewish people as a whole when he wrote:

"Yet there is one ray of hope: his compassion never ends. It is only the Lord's mercies that have kept us from complete destruction. Great is his faithfulness; his loving-kindness begins fresh each day. My soul claims the Lord as my inheritance; therefore I will hope in him. The Lord is wonderfully good to those who wait for him, to those who seek for him. It is good to hope and wait quietly for the salvation of the Lord" (Lamentations 3:21-26 TLB).

God's love is also *infinite.* This means it has no limits or bounds. It cannot be measured. Human love is constantly fluctuating. Sometimes we love someone more than we do at other times. Then sometimes we love them less. This is because our love is influenced by the object of our love. We love people more or less in relationship to their response to us.

But God's love is different. He doesn't add or take away from His love. He doesn't love us more at times than He does at other times. Nor does He love us less at times. This means there is nothing the Jewish people can do to earn God's love. There is no good work they can do to make God love them any more than He already does. Neither is there any evil they can do that would make Him love them any less. God loves the Jewish people today just as much as He did when He brought them out of Egypt and confirmed His covenant with them through Moses. For a beautiful description of the infinite love of God, I suggest you read Ezekiel 16.

Finally, God's love is *uncaused*. When we love someone it's because we find something we believe to be lovable in the one we love. We see something in another person that calls forth our love. That person becomes the object of our love.

But God's love is different. God's love is uncaused. God does not love out of passion or emotion. God loves because love is who God is.

God loves the unlovable as well as the lovable. In fact, in God's eyes, all of us are unlovable. This is because we have all sinned and come short of His glory. The Jewish people have sinned by turning away from God and breaking their commitment to the covenant God made with them. They sinned by rejecting their Messiah. But God still loves them.

God loves the Jewish people with a holy, eternal, infinite, uncaused love. And because God loves them, we who claim to know God should also love them.

4. Love Is The Mark Of A Christian

Christians should love the Jewish people because love is the mark of a true Christian. Jesus said, "By this all will know that you are My disciples, if you have love for one another" (John 13:35 NKJ).

Jesus further added, "As the Father loved Me, I also have loved you; abide in My love. If you keep My commandments you will abide in My love, just as I have kept My Father's commandments and abide in His love. . .This is My commandment, that you love one another as I have loved you. Greater love has no one than this, than to lay down one's life for his friend" (John 15:9-13 NKJ).

Jesus said the greatest way we can express our love for another is by giving our life for that person. Jesus set this example by giving His life for us. We Christians may find

163

that we will have to give our life to save the life of a Jewish person. If you are called upon to do so, you will be showing that Jewish person the heart of Christianity. By doing so, you will be pointing him to Messiah Jesus who gave His life for the sins of Jew and Gentile alike.

The apostle John wrote about the need for true Christian love. He said, "My little children, let us not love in word or in tongue, but in deed and in truth" (1 John 3:18 NKJ).

He then added, "No one has seen God at any time. If we love one another, God abides in us, and His love has been perfected in us. And we have known and believed the love that God has for us. God is love, and he who abides in love abides in God, and God in him. If someone says, "I love God," and hates his brother, he is a liar; for he who does not love his brother whom he has seen, how can he love God whom he has not seen? And this commandment we have from Him: that he who loves God must love his brother also" (1 John 4:12,16,20-21 NKJ).

When the Jewish people see true Christian love, it will be a witness to them that God loves them and desires that they respond to His love. Many will turn to Him and acknowledge Jesus as their Messiah. *This will not happen because Christians have beaten the Jews over the head with the gospel, but because we will have shown them that the love of God has been placed in our hearts through Messiah Jesus.*

5. The Jews Need Our Love

Finally, Christians should show love to the Jewish people because they need our love. As we've learned in this book, the Jewish people have historically suffered much at the hands of the Gentile nations. Today, Israel's only friend, the United States, is wavering in its support of the Jewish nation. In the future, we've learned, that all nations will come against Israel.

Anti-semitism is once again becoming justifiable and acceptable. We can expect an increase in anti-Jewish sentiment and actions. The Jewish period of tribulation is near when the Gentile nations of the world will vent their anger

164

and frustration against the Jews. There will be great persecution as we've already discussed. Millions of Jews will be killed. Jerusalem will be temporarily occupied by the Antichrist and his armies.

For these reasons, the Jewish people need Christians to stand with them against their persecutors. They need Christians to show them the love of Messiah Jesus. They need Christians to comfort them and encourage them in the faithfulness of God to keep His covenant promises to them.

Perhaps you have not shown love to the Jewish people as you should. I pray that you will ask God to forgive you of any past attitudes or actions which have been unpleasing to Him in this regard. Then begin to pray for Israel as a nation and for Jewish people everywhere. Pray that they will turn their hearts toward God. Pray for their protection. Then when possible, demonstrate your love for them through works of loving-kindness.

For my Jewish friends who may be reading this book, I encourage you with the reminder that God loves you. He has not forsaken you. He will not forsake you. He has carved you on the palm of His hand. You are not alone. True Christian believers around the world also love you and are praying for you. We are praying for the peace of Jerusalem.

Scripture References

God speaks of the need for love to both Jew and Gentile in the following Scriptures:

"You shall not take vengeance, nor bear any grudge against the children of your people, but you shall love your neighbor as yourself: I am the LORD" (Leviticus 19:18 NKJ).

"But the stranger who dwells among you shall be to you as one born among you, and you shall love him as yourself; for you were strangers in the land of Egypt: I am the LORD your God" (Leviticus 19:34 NKJ).

"Therefore love the stranger, for you were strangers in the land of Egypt" (Deuteronomy 10:19 NKJ).

"You have heard that it was said, 'You shall love your neighbor and hate your enemy.' But I say to you, love your enemies, bless those who curse you, do good to those who hate you, and pray for those who spitefully use you and persecute you, that you may be sons of your Father in heaven; for He makes His sun rise on the evil and on the good, and sends rain on the just and on the unjust. . . For if you love those who love you, what reward have you? Do not even the tax collectors do the same? And if you greet your brethren only, what do you do more than others? Do not even the tax collectors do so? Therefore you shall be perfect, just as your Father in heaven is perfect" (Matthew 5:43-48 NKJ).

" 'Teacher, which is the great commandment in the law?' Jesus said to him, 'You shall love the LORD your God with all your heart, with all your soul, and with all your mind.' This is the first and great commandment. And the second is like it: 'You shall love your neighbor as yourself.' On these two commandments hang all the Law and the Prophets" (Matthew 22:36-40 NKJ).

"A new commandment I give to you, that you love one another; as I have loved you, that you also love one another. By this all will know that you are My disciples, if you have love for one another" (John 13:34-35 NKJ).

"Owe no one anything except to love one another, for he who loves another has fulfilled the law. . . Love does no harm to a neighbor; therefore love is the fulfillment of the law" (Romans 13:8,10 NKJ).

"For you, brethren, have been called to liberty; only do not use liberty as an opportunity for the flesh, but through love serve one another. For all the law is fulfilled in one word, even in this: 'You shall love your neighbor as yourself' " (Galatians 5:13-14 NKJ).

"Beloved, let us love one another, for love is of God; and everyone who loves is born of God and knows

God. He who does not love does not know God, for God is love" (1 John 4:7-8 NKJ).

"If someone says, 'I love God,' and hates his brother, he is a liar; for he who does not love his brother whom he has seen, how can he love God whom he has not seen? And this commandment we have from Him: that he who loves God must love his brother also" (1 John 4:20-21 NKJ).

Chapter 15—Why Christians Should Love Jews

Study Guide 14

1. List five reasons why Christians should love Jews.

   a. We owe them a debt

   b. They provided us with the Bible
   → They need our love

   c. They provided us with Morality
   → Abraham is our father

   d. God loves them

   e. Love is the Mark of a Christian

2. Explain how Christians are "spiritual Jews."

We have been circumsised (heart)
We are God's People

16

How To Recognize The Jewish Messiah

One point I've tried to make in this book is that the center of the Jewish faith is the teaching concerning the Messiah. As previously noted, the Hebrew Scriptures speak of a personal deliverer who would be sent by God for the purpose of ruling Israel and the nations of the earth with justice and righteousness. He would usher in the golden age about which the prophets spoke.

It was God's desire that the Jewish people be able to recognize the Messiah when He came on the scene. To help them do so, *God gave many details about the Messiah to the prophets who passed this information on to the people.* These prophecies provided the necessary details about the birth, life, death and rule of the Messiah to enable the Jewish people to recognize Him.

Two Portraits of Messiah

However, as the rabbis studied these prophecies, they become somewhat confused over what seemed to be a contradiction. There were some prophecies that spoke about the Messiah as being a great king and deliverer who would destroy the enemies of Israel and establish her as the head nation of the earth. In other words, He would be a *political-military Messiah*.

On the other hand, there were also prophecies that spoke about the Messiah as being a humble and gentle teacher who would suffer greatly and be put to death, bearing the sins of the people and making atonement for them before God. These prophecies were descriptions of a *religious Messiah*.

The Messianic Puzzle

The two portraits of the Messiah were very clear. But what was not clear was how both could be speaking about the same person. The greatest scholars could not harmonize these two seemingly contradictory portraits of the Messiah.

Some scholars thought that perhaps two Messiahs would come. One Messiah would be the political-military ruler while the other would be the religious leader. The political-military Messiah would establish the kingdom of David and bring to pass the nationalistic promises in the Abrahamic covenant. The religious Messiah would establish the kingdom of God and put into effect the spiritual promises of the Abrahamic covenant.

This is exactly what the previously mentioned Antichrist and False Prophet will attempt to establish during the tribulation period. However, it will be a counterfeit. Unfortunately, many Jews will be deceived by their trickery.

Messianic Tunnel Vision

For centuries, the Jews looked for the coming of the Messiah. As time passed, they found themselves subjected to one Gentile power after another. There was Assyria, Babylon, Medo-Persia, Greece and finally Rome. They longed to be free from foreign domination. In view of this, they naturally focused their attention on the prophecies that spoke about the Messiah as the great Deliverer. They wanted a political-military Messiah who would overthrow the Romans and restore the sovereignty of Israel as a nation.

As a result, they naturally tended to ignore the prophecies that spoke of the Messiah as a religious leader. They had had enough of suffering, persecution and death. The rabbis no longer spoke of this role of the Messiah. They told the people what they wanted to hear. After a time, generations of young Jews only knew the political-military portrait of the Messiah. They had Messianic tunnel vision in that they could only see this one view of the Messiah. This was the situation during the time of Jesus of Nazareth.

One Messiah—Two Comings

What the rabbis were not able to understand was that both portraits of the Messiah would be fulfilled in one person, but not at the same time. There would be a time gap between the two roles the Messiah would play. This would require Him to appear on planet earth at two different times. The first time He would come as the religious Messiah to bring atonement for sin and establish the spiritual realm of the kingdom of God in the hearts of men. Then after a period of time, He would come again as the political-military Messiah to establish the physical kingdom of God over all the earth and the physical kingdom of David to administer it along with the resurrected believers of all ages. This is the Messianic kingdom which we learned about in chapter fourteen.

A chart is provided at the end of this chapter entitled, "How To Recognize The Jewish Messiah." This chart highlights the prophecies we are now going to discuss and provides a snapshot of the two portraits of the Messiah. You may want to look over this chart before continuing in your reading. Then after you've finished reading the chapter, you may find it helpful to record the corresponding Hebrew and New Testament Scriptures in the margin of your Bible.

171

Hebrew Scriptures and Jesus Of Nazareth

As a Christian, I believe that the Hebrew Scriptures were pointing to Jesus of Nazareth as the fulfillment of both of these portraits of the Messiah. At this time, we are going to examine these two portraits of the Messiah from the Hebrew Scriptures and then compare them to the New Testament witness to Jesus. As we do, it is my earnest prayer that my Jewish friends will see the connection between the Hebrew Scriptures and Jesus and acknowledge Him as their Messiah.

The following comparison is not intended to be an exhaustive study of the subject. These are simply some of the more obvious Scriptures that highlight key prophecies in the Hebrew Scriptures concerning the two portraits of the Messiah and how they relate to Jesus.

1. The Messiah's Birth

The first information the Jews needed to have about their Messiah pertained to His birth. The Hebrew Scriptures told the place, manner and time of the Messiah's birth as well as giving His ancestry.

A. *Place Of Birth*

God gave the prophet Micah the wonderful privilege of foretelling the birthplace of the Messiah. He made the prediction about 750 years prior to the time the Messiah would be born in the little Judean town of *Bethlehem*. He wrote, "But you, Bethlehem Ephrathah, though you are little among the thousands of Judah, Yet out of you shall come forth to Me The One to be ruler in Israel, Whose goings forth have been from old, From everlasting" (Micah 5:2 NKJ).

According to the New Testament Scriptures, *Jesus was born in Bethlehem.* Matthew wrote, "NOW WHEN Jesus was born in Bethlehem of Judea in the days of Herod the king. . ." (Matthew 2:1 KJV).

It's most interesting how Jesus came to be born in Bethlehem. His mother and stepfather lived in Nazareth. But the Roman ruler, Caesar Augustus, had decreed a special tax on his conquered subjects, including the Jews. This special tax was to be collected through a census which was to require the people to return to the birthplace of their ancestry. Since both Mary and Joseph were descendants of King David, they were to go to Bethlehem, the birthplace of David.

Their journey to Bethlehem was delayed until after Mary became pregnant and was near the time for her to give birth. This delay was caused by the Jewish leaders filing a protest against the tax, which the Romans denied. But it took time for the news that the protest had been denied to reach the area where Joseph and Mary lived. When the news finally did come, Joseph and Mary journeyed to Bethlehem just in time for Jesus to be born.

Now you may think these circumstances and the particular timing problems associated with them were a coincidence. That is your privilege. I choose to believe it was God moving events to bring to pass the birth of Jesus in Bethlehem to fulfill the ancient prophecy given by Micah.

B. Manner of Birth

No doubt the most amazing prophecy concerning the Messiah related to the manner of His birth. Isaiah prophecied about the same time as Micah that the Messiah would be *born of a virgin.* Isaiah said, "Therefore the Lord himself shall give you a sign; Behold a virgin shall conceive, and bear a son, and shall call his name Immanuel" (Isaiah 7:14 KJV).

When you think about it, any human birth is a fantastic miracle. But the birth of the Messiah was to be an even bigger miracle than normal birth. The Messiah would be born of a virgin. This supernatural birth was to be a special sign from God pointing the Jews to one particular baby born in Bethlehem.

Some scholars of the Hebrew Scriptures have pointed out that the Hebrew word "almah" which is translated into the English word "virgin" can also be translated to mean a "young maiden." This would refer to an unmarried young

173

woman. However, this translation would be meaningless as a sign because unfortunately many unmarried young women had children. That would not be so unusual for Isaiah to call it a sign. But a miraculous virgin birth would certainly be a sign from heaven to help the Jewish people recognize their Messiah.

I might also point out that 250 years before Jesus was born the Jews translated the Hebrew Scriptures into Greek. When they came to Isaiah 7:14, they translated the word "almah" into the Greek word "parthenos." This Greek word means "virgin." The Jews were looking for a virgin-born Messiah.

Isaiah went on to say that this virgin-born Messiah would be called "Immanuel." The word Immanuel means "God with us!" Isaiah considered the Messiah to be more than just a human superman. He would be God Himself taking on human form.

Isaiah further declared the divine nature of the Messiah with these words, "For unto us a child is born, unto us a son is given: and the government shall be upon his shoulder: and his name shall be called Wonderful, Counsellor, The Mighty God, The Everlasting Father, The Prince of Peace" (Isaiah 9:6 KJV).

Micah also made this connection when he prophecied about the Messiah being born in Bethlehem. He said the Messiah would be One whose goings forth have been from of old, from everlasting. Micah could only be speaking about God Himself.

We learn from these and many other Hebrew Scriptures that the Messiah would be more than just a human of extraordinary abilities. He would actually be God Himself coming to live in the midst of His people.

The New Testament scriptures state that *Jesus was born of a virgin.* The angel Gabriel was given the mission of announcing His birth. Luke the physician recorded the following account of that dramatic announcement. He wrote, "Now in the sixth month the angel Gabriel was sent by God to a city of Galilee named Nazareth, to a virgin betrothed to

174

a man whose name was Joseph, of the house of David. The virgin's name was Mary. And having come in, the angel said to her, 'Rejoice, highly favored one, the Lord is with you; blessed are you among women!' But when she saw him, she was troubled at his saying, and considered what manner of greeting this was. Then the angel said to her, 'Do not be afraid, Mary, for you have found favor with God. And behold, you will conceive in your womb and bring forth a Son, and shall call His name Jesus' " (Luke 1:26-31 NKJ).

This, of course, was a very startling announcement to Mary. She knew she had never had sexual relations with Joseph nor any other man. She asked the natural question which Gabriel then answered. Luke wrote, "Then Mary said to the angel, 'How can this be, since I do not know a man?' And the angel answered and said unto her, 'The Holy Spirit will come upon you, and the power of the Highest will overshadow you; therefore, also, that Holy One who is to be born will be called the Son of God' " (Luke 1:34-35 NKJ).

When it became obvious that Mary was pregnant, Joseph was devastated and hurt. He naturally believed that Mary had been unfaithful to him. He felt betrayed. God used an angel to comfort Joseph in a dream and explain what was taking place in Mary's body. Matthew wrote, "Now the birth of Jesus Christ was as follows: After His mother Mary was betrothed to Joseph, before they came together, she was found with child of the Holy Spirit. Then Joseph her husband, being a just man, and not wanting to make her a public example, was minded to put her away secretly. But while he thought about these things, behold, an angel of the Lord appeared to him in a dream, saying, 'Joseph, son of David, do not be afraid to take to you Mary your wife, for that which is conceived in her is of the Holy Spirit. And she will bring forth a Son, and you shall call His name Jesus, for He will save His people from their sins' " (Matthew 1:18-21 NKJ).

Matthew then went on to explain that this was the fulfillment of the prophecy given by Isaiah. He said, "Now all this was done that it might be fulfilled which was spoken by the

Lord through the prophet saying, 'Behold a virgin shall be with child, and bear a Son, and they shall call His name Immanuel, which is translated, 'God with us' " (Matthew 1:22-23 NKJ).

C. Time Of Birth

To further help the Jews recognize the first coming of their Messiah, God gave them information pertaining to the time period when He would be born. We read in Genesis 49:10, "The scepter shall not depart from Judah, nor a lawgiver from between his feet until Shiloh come; and unto him shall the gathering of the people be (NKJ)."

In this scripture reference, Jacob is giving his blessings to his sons just prior to his death. The blessing which he gives to Judah is that Judah's descendants will be the kings of Israel. Jacob then prophecies that Judah's descendants would rule over Israel as a nation until Shiloh comes. But after Shiloh comes, the national sovereignty and identity of Israel will be taken away and given to another.

The word Shiloh means "to whom it rightfully belongs." The Jews considered this to be a reference to the Messiah who had the ultimate right to rule over Israel. According to Jacob's words, *the Messiah must come before Israel loses her nation's sovereignty and identity to another.*

As we've learned in earlier chapters, Israel lost her national identity in 70 AD to the Romans. They were driven from the land and scattered among the nations.*Whoever the Messiah was, He had to come in the first century before the dissolution of the nation of Israel and their subsequent dispersion. Jesus is the only possible candidate who can meet this requirement as He was born, lived and died in the first century prior to the events of 70 AD.*

D. Messiah's Ancestry

In chapter three, we learned that God chose David as the royal family through whom the Messiah would come. God spoke these words to David through the prophet Nathan, "And it shall be, when your days are fulfilled, when you must go to be with your fathers, that I will set up your seed after you, who will be of your sons; and I will establish his kingdom. He shall build Me a house, and I will establish his throne forever. I will be his Father, and he shall be My son; and I will not take My mercy away from him, as I took it from him who was before you. And I will establish him in My house and in My kingdom forever; and his throne shall be established forever" (1 Chronicles 17:11-14 NKJ).

God promised David that he would have a descendant who would rule the nation of Israel forever. The Jews recognized this "greater Son of David" to be the Messiah. Therefore, the Messiah had to be a descendant of David.

The New Testament Scriptures tell us that *Jesus was a descendant of David*. When Gabriel made the announcement to Mary that she would give birth to Jesus, he referred to God's promise to David and said that it was fulfilled in Jesus. Luke reads, "And behold, you will conceive in your womb and bring forth a Son, and shall call His name Jesus. He will be great, and will be called the Son of the Highest; and the Lord God will give Him the throne of His father David. And He will reign over the house of Jacob forever, and of His kingdom there will be no end" (Luke 1:31-33 NKJ).

We see clearly that the Hebrew Scriptures foretold the coming of the Messiah. He would be God Himself coming into the world through a supernatural birth. He would be born in Bethlehem as a descendant of David and live prior to 70 AD. Jesus met all of these qualifications so that through the prophecies concerning the Messiah's birth, any honest seeker can recognize Him as the One to whom they were pointing.

2. The Messiah's Life And Ministry

God not only foretold the events surrounding the birth of the Messiah, He also provided many details concerning His life and ministry. God wanted the Jewish people to be able to clearly recognize the Messiah. There was to be no doubt. Let's now take a look at some of the more obvious prophe-

177

cies in the Hebrew Scriptures concerning the life and ministry of the Messiah and see how Jesus fulfilled each of them.

A. Heralded By A Forerunner

One of the key ways the Messiah could be recognized was that He was to be *preceded by a forerunner* who would announce His coming and point the people to Him. In ancient times, kings and dignitaries were preceded by a herald who proclaimed his coming so that the people would be prepared to greet him. The same was true for the Messiah—the king of the Jews.

Two prophets spoke of this forerunner—Isaiah and Malachi. Isaiah was the first to prophesy of his special role of introducing the Messiah about 750 years prior to His ministry. He wrote, "The voice of one crying in the wilderness: 'Prepare the way of the LORD; Make straight in the desert a highway for our God' " (Isaiah 40:3 NKJ).

Isaiah spoke of this forerunner as "the voice crying in the wilderness." As we carefully read Isaiah's words, we see that the voice in the wilderness would prepare the people to receive the LORD. When the english word "LORD" appears in all capital letters in the King James Version of the Bible, it is a reference to Jehovah. Isaiah substantiates this by connecting the word LORD to God. This is just one of many Hebrew Scriptures that identify the Messiah as God Himself.

Malachi confirmed Isaiah's prediction of the forerunner about 350 years later. God spoke these words through Malachi, "Behold, I send My messenger, And he will prepare the way before Me. And the Lord, whom you seek, Will suddenly come to His temple, Even the Messenger of the covenant, In whom you delight. Behold, He is coming, says the LORD of hosts" (Malachi 3:1 NKJ).

We notice in Malachi's prophecy that the forerunner is to prepare the way for *God*. We also observe that in Malachi's statement, the word "Lord" is used in reference to the Messiah. When the word "Lord" appears in lower case letters in the King James Version of the Bible it is a reference to God as King rather than to God's name—Jehovah. This is another instance where the Hebrew Scriptures tell us that *the Messiah-King is none other than Jehovah God.*

Malachi further spoke about the forerunner to the Messiah and identified Him with Elijah the prophet (Malachi 4:5). For this reason, the Jews have expected Elijah, who never died, to return and announce the coming of the Messiah.

The New Testament Scriptures tell us of a forerunner to Jesus who announced His coming and did his best to prepare the people to receive Him. This forerunner was known as John the Baptist.

Matthew wrote that John the Baptist was the one about whom Isaiah and Malachi were speaking. He said, "In those days John the Baptist came preaching in the wilderness of Judea, and saying, 'Repent, for the kingdom of heaven is at hand!' For this is he who was spoken of by the prophet Isaiah, saying: 'The voice of one crying in the wilderness: Prepare the way of the LORD, Make His paths straight' " (Matthew 3:1-3 NKJ).

Luke also wrote about John the Baptist and said that he was the one Malachi spoke about when he identified the forerunner to the Messiah as Elijah. Luke explains that Malachi was not necessarily speaking about Elijah himself, but one who would preach with the same anointing of God as Elijah had preached.

Luke says of John the Baptist, "And he will turn many of the children of Israel to the Lord their God. He will also go before Him in the spirit and power of Elijah, 'to turn the hearts of the fathers to the children,' and the disobedient to the wisdom of the just, to make ready a people prepared for the Lord" (Luke 1:16-17 NKJ).

Jesus identified John the Baptist as the one whom Isaiah and Malachi were speaking about. He said of John, "This is he of whom it is written: 'Behold, I send My messenger before your face, Who will prepare Your way before You' " (Luke 7:27 NKJ).

As Jesus' disciples acknowledged Him as the Messiah,

they asked Him about Malachi's prophecy concerning Elijah. They were wondering, in view of their acceptance of Jesus as Messiah, why Elijah had not come to announce Jesus to the people. Jesus responded to their question by again identifying John the Baptist as the one Malchi was speaking about.

Matthew wrote, "Then Jesus answered and said to them, 'Elijah is truly coming first and will restore all things. But I say to you that Elijah has come already, and they did not know him but did to him whatever they wished. Likewise the Son of Man is also about to suffer at their hands.' Then the disciples understood that He spoke to them of John the Baptist" (Matthew 17:11-13 NKJ).

As we've learned, the Messiah was to establish the kingdom of God on planet earth. The forerunner would prepare the people to receive Him. John the Baptist was a "type" of Elijah in that he preached in the spirit and power of Elijah. *If the Jewish people would have received Jesus as their Messiah, God would have considered John the Baptist to be the complete fulfillment of Malachi's prophecy.*

Jesus said of John's message, "And if you are willing to receive it, he is Elijah who is to come" (Matthew 11:14 NKJ).

B. Minister To The Poor And Needy

Isaiah predicted that the Messiah would not only be a great leader, but that He would also be *a man of compassion who would minister to the poor and needy.* Isaiah said these words concerning the Messiah, "The Spirit of the Lord God is upon Me, Because the LORD has anointed Me To preach good tidings to the poor; He has sent Me to heal the brokenhearted, To proclaim liberty to the captives, And the opening of the prison to those who are bound; To proclaim the acceptable year of the LORD. . ." (Isaiah 61:1-2 NKJ).

Jesus began His ministry in His hometown of Galilee. It was His custom to go to the Synagogue on the Sabbath. On one particular Sabbath, He stood up to read the Scriptures.

180

The place from which He read was the prophecy by Isaiah concerning the Messiah.

Luke recorded this event for us and wrote, "So He came to Nazareth, where He had been brought up. And as His custom was, He went into the synagogue on the Sabbath day, and stood up to read. And He was handed the book of the prophet Isaiah. And when He had opened the book, He found the place where it was written 'The Spirit of the LORD is upon Me, Because He has anointed Me to preach the gospel to the poor. He has sent Me to heal the broken-hearted, To preach deliverance to the captives And recovery of sight to the blind, To set at liberty those who are oppressed, To preach the acceptable year of the LORD' " (Luke 4:16-19 NKJ).

After Jesus read this, He gave the book back to the attendant and sat down. Jesus had gotten the attention of the crowd. All eyes were fixed on Him. He wanted them to know His purpose for reading Isaiah's prophecy. He turned to them and said, ". . . Today this scripture is fulfilled in your hearing" (Luke 4:21 NKJ).

Jesus was boldly claiming to be the fulfillment of Isaiah's prophecy. He was publicly declaring that He was their long-awaited-for Messiah who had come, not just to establish a kingdom with power and glory, but also to minister to the poor and needy. As we follow His ministry in the gospel records, we see that He made Himself available to the common people and those who were hurting and suffering the most from the problems and pressures of life.

C. Worker Of Miracles

Isaiah gave further information about the Messiah to help the Jews recognize Him. Isaiah said the Messiah would be a *miracle worker.* We read the following prophetic description, "Say to those who are fearful-hearted, 'Be strong, do not fear! Behold, your God will come with vengeance, With the recompense of God; he will come and save you.' Then the eyes of the blind shall be opened, And the ears of the deaf shall be unstopped. Then the lame shall leap like a

181

deer, And the tongue of the dumb sing. . ." (Isaiah 35:4-6 NKJ).

Once again we turn to the New Testament Scriptures and see that *Jesus was a worker of miracles.* He healed the sick, made the lame to walk, opened blind eyes and deaf ears, loosened the tongues of those who could not speak, cleansed the lepers and raised the dead.

Jesus performed these miracles for the purpose of establishing His authenticity as the Messiah. Anybody could claim to be the Messiah, and many did. But the quickest way to expose a fraud was to see if the person performed miracles. The miracles which Jesus performed were His credentials that established the genuineness of His claims.

John the Baptist had been given the death sentence by King Herod. While he was waiting for his execution, he wanted one last word of encouragement from Jesus. He knew that Jesus was also to die because he had introduced Jesus as the lamb of God who had come to take away the sins of the world (John 1:29). But he was still somewhat confused as to how one man could fulfill both portraits of the Messiah. Perhaps John wanted to know if Jesus was the complete fulfillment of all the prophecies concerning the Messiah, or if there would be two Messiahs, one religious and one political. He sent two of his followers to ask Jesus this question in order to clear up his confusion. They asked Jesus, ". . . Are You the coming One, or do we look for another?" (Matthew 11:3 NKJ)

Jesus did not give them a direct yes or no answer. He did something even better. Instead of asking John just to take His word, Jesus told John's followers to go and tell John about the miracles they were seeing Jesus perform. He said, ". . . Go and tell John the things which you hear and see: The blind receive their sight and the lame walk; the lepers are cleansed and the deaf hear; the dead are raised up and the poor have the gospel preached to them. And blessed is he who is not offended because of Me" (Matthew 11:4-6 NKJ).

Jesus connected His ministry to Isaiah's prophecy and in

doing so was claiming to be the Messiah based on the miracles that He performed.

After one of Jesus' sermons, the Jews came to Him and demanded, ". . . How long do You keep us in doubt? If you are the Christ, tell us plainly" (John 10:24 NKJ). Jesus answered them by saying that the miracles He performed gave credibility to His other claims verifying that He indeed was the Messiah.

D. Acknowledged By Many

The Hebrew Scriptures said that the Messiah would come to Jerusalem riding on a donkey and be *acknowledged by many* as their king. The prophet Zechariah spoke these words, "Rejoice greatly, O daughter of Zion! Shout, O daughter of Jerusalem! Behold, your King is coming to you; He is just and having salvation, Lowly and riding on a donkey, A colt, the foal of a donkey" (Zechariah 9:9 NKJ).

Matthew recorded that Jesus rode into Jerusalem on a donkey and was acknowledged by many of the Jews as their king. Matthew connected this action by Jesus to Zechariah's prophecy to show that Jesus was the Messiah.

Matthew wrote, "All this was done that it might be fulfilled which was spoken by the prophet, saying: 'Tell the daughter of Zion, Behold, your King is coming to you, Lowly and sitting on a donkey, A colt, the foal of a donkey.' " So the disciples went and did as Jesus commanded them. They brought the donkey and the colt, laid their clothes on them, and set Him on them. And a very great multitude spread their garments on the road; others cut down branches from the trees and spread them on the road. Then the multitudes who went before and those who cried out, saying: 'Hosanna to the Son of David! Blessed is He who comes in the name of the LORD! Hosanna in the highest' " (Matthew 21:4-9 NKJ).

After Jesus' resurrection, the apostle Peter preached to large crowds of Jews concerning the Messiahship of Jesus. Of those attending his first sermon, three thousand Jews accepted Jesus as their Messiah (Acts 2:41). This number quickly grew to five thousand (Acts 4:4), and soon many more came to recognize Jesus as the long-awaited-for Messiah (Acts 5:42).

E. Rejected By Most

Isaiah often spoke about the glory of Israel under the rule of the Messiah. But he also said that the *Messiah would be rejected by the nation as a whole.* Isaiah wrote these words about the Messiah, "He is despised and rejected by men, A man of sorrows and acquainted with grief. And we hid, as it were, our faces from Him; He was despised, and we did not esteem Him" (Isaiah 53:3 NKJ).

Although many Jews accepted Jesus as their Messiah, most rejected Him. Those who rejected Jesus followed Him for awhile. But they soon grew impatient with His talk of sin and the need for repentance. When they saw that Jesus was not going to lead them in a revolt against Rome, they rejected Him.

Matthew gave the following account, "Now at the feast the governor was accustomed to releasing to the multitude one prisoner whom they wished. And they had then a notorious prisoner called Barabbas. Therefore, when they had gathered together, Pilate said to them, 'Whom do you want me to release to you? Barabbas, or Jesus who is called Christ?' For he knew that because of envy they had delivered Him. While he was sitting on the judgement seat, his wife sent to him, saying, 'Have nothing to do with that just Man, for I have suffered many things today in a dream because of Him.' But the chief priests and elders persuaded the multitudes that they should ask for Barabbas and destroy Jesus. The governor answered and said to them, 'Which of the two do you want me to release to you?' They said, 'Barabbas!' Pilate said to them, 'What then shall I do with Jesus who is called Christ?' They all said to him, 'Let Him be crucified!' Then the governor said, 'Why, what evil has He done?' But they cried out all the more, saying, 'Let Him be crucified!' When Pilate saw that he could not prevail at all, but rather that a tumult was rising, he took water and washed his hands before the multitude, saying, 'I an innocent of the blood of this just Person. You see to it.' And all the people answered and said, 'His blood be on us and on our children.' Then he released Barabbas to them; and when he had scourged Jesus, he delivered Him to be crucified" (Matthew 27:15-26 NKJ).

3. The Messiah's Suffering

As we've noted, the Hebrew Scriptures gave two contrasting portraits of the Messiah. He was to be a powerful leader as well as a humble teacher who would experience great suffering. Before the Messiah could assume His role as the King of the Jews and the King of Kings, He first had to suffer as the lamb of God who would take away their sins and the sins of the world. We now are going to briefly highlight a few Hebrew Scriptures that spoke of the Messiah's suffering and then see how they relate to Jesus of Nazareth.

A. His Betrayal

Let's begin with the Messiah's betrayal. One of King David's most trusted advisors was a man by the name of Ahithophel. Ahithophel was David's closest confidant and friend. Yet he betrayed David by becoming part of a conspiracy against him. When the conspiracy failed, Ahithophel hanged himself (2 Samuel 17:1-23).

David wrote of his friend's betrayal, "Even my own familiar friend in whom I trusted, Who ate my bread, Has lifted up his heel against me" (Psalm 41:9 NKJ).

When we come to the New Testament Scriptures, we find Jesus referring to David's statement in Psalms and applying it to His own imminent betrayal by Judas.

It was at the last passover meal that Jesus had with His disciples when He said, "I do not speak concerning all of you. I know whom I have chosen; but that the Scripture may be fulfilled, 'He who eats bread with Me has lifted up his heel against Me.' . . . When Jesus had said these things, He was troubled in spirit, and testified and said, 'Most assuredly, I say to you, one of you will betray Me' " (John 13:18,21 NKJ).

As we might expect, the disciples were very troubled by Jesus' statement. They ask Him who it was who would betray Him. Jesus replied, " '. . . It is he to whom I shall give a piece of bread when I have dipped it.' " And having dipped the bread, He gave it to Judas Iscariot, the son of Simon" (John 13:26 NKJ).

As with King David, Jesus was also betrayed by His very close friend who hanged himself. Incredibly, the Hebrew Scriptures further stated the exact price for which the Messiah would be betrayed and what would become of the "blood money."

The prophet Zechariah wrote, " '. . . If it is agreeable to you, give me my wages; and if not, refrain.' So they weighed out for my wages thirty pieces of silver. And the LORD said to me, 'Throw it to the potter—that princely price they set on me.' So I took the thirty pieces of silver and threw them into the house of the LORD for the potter" (Zechariah 11:12-13 NKJ).

Zechariah prophesied about 500 years prior to the birth of Jesus that the Messiah would be betrayed for thirty pieces of silver and that the money would be thrown down in the house of the LORD (the temple), and used to purchase a burial plot in which to bury strangers (the potter's field).

Judas betrayed Jesus for thirty pieces of silver. Matthew said, "Then one of the twelve, called Judas Iscariot, went to the chief priests and said, 'What are you willing to give me if I deliver Him to you?' And they counted out to him thirty pieces of silver. So from that time he sought opportunity to betray Him" (Matthew 26:14-16 NKJ).

When Judas saw how badly Jesus had been beaten and that He was going to be killed, he had second thoughts about betraying Jesus. He experienced such heavy guilt that he decided if he returned the thirty pieces of silver, perhaps his burden would be lifted. He went back to the religious leaders who had given the money and confessed that he had betrayed an innocent man. He asked them to take the money back, but they refused. Then in fulfillment of Zechariah's prophecy, Judas threw the money down in the temple and went and hanged himself.

Matthew recorded this as follows, "Then Judas, his betrayer, seeing that He had been condemned, was remorseful and brought back the thirty pieces of silver to the chief priests and elders, saying, 'I have sinned by betraying innocent blood.' And they said, 'What is that to us? You see to it!' Then he threw down the pieces of silver in the temple and departed, and went and hanged himself" (Matthew 27:3-5 NKJ).

This presented the religious leaders with a problem. It was against Jewish law for them to put this blood money back into the temple treasury. But they did have an option to spend it for the public good. One of the ways they could use this money for the public good was to purchase a burial plot to bury strangers. Isn't that interesting?

The religious leaders used the money to purchase a burial plot in the potters field just as Zechariah had predicted. Matthew went on to write, "But the chief priests took the silver pieces and said, 'It is not lawful to put them into the treasury, because they are the price of blood.' And they took counsel and bought with them the potter's field, to bury strangers in" (Matthew 27:6-7 NKJ).

B. His Trials

The Hebrew Scriptures also spoke much about the Messiah's trials. We learn in the Psalms that the *Messiah was to be falsely accused.* Psalms 35:11-12 reads, "False witnesses did rise up; they laid to my charge things I knew not. They rewarded me evil for good to the spoiling of my soul" (KJV).

Jesus was falsely accused. Matthew wrote, "Now the chief priests, the elders, and all the council sought false testimony against Jesus to put Him to death, but found none. But at last two false witnesses came forward" (Matthew 26:59-60 NKJ).

Isaiah prophesied that the *Messiah would keep silent before His false accusers and not defend Himself.* Isaiah reads, "He was oppressed and He was afflicted, Yet He opened not

187

His mouth; He was led as a lamb to the slaughter, And as a sheep before its shearers is silent, So He opened not his mouth" (Isaiah 53:7 NKJ).

Likewise, Jesus was silent before His accusers. Matthew tells us, "And while He was being accused by the chief priests and elders, He answered nothing. Then Pilate said to Him, 'Do you not hear how many things they testify against you?' And He answered him not one word, so that the governor marveled greatly" (Matthew 27:12-14 NKJ).

Both Isaiah and Micah said that the *Messiah would be struck and spat on.* Isaiah wrote these words concerning the Messiah, "I gave My back to those who struck Me. . ." (Isaiah 50:6 NKJ). He then added, "Surely He has borne our griefs And carried our sorrows; Yet we esteemed Him stricken, Smitten by God, and afflicted. . .For the transgressions of My people He was stricken" (Isaiah 53:4,8 NKJ).

Micah also prophesied this with these words, ". . . They will strike the judge of Israel with a rod on the cheek" (Micah 5:1 NKJ).

As we examine the trials of Jesus, we see that He was struck and spat on. Matthew reads, "Then they spat on His face and beat Him; and others struck Him with the palms of their hands" (Matthew 26:67 NKJ).

Isaiah wrote that the *Messiah would be wounded and bruised,* "But He was wounded for our transgressions, He was bruised for our iniquities; The chastisement for our peace was upon Him; And by His stripes we are healed. All we like sheep have gone astray; We have turned, every one, to his own way; And the LORD has laid on Him the iniquity of us all" (Isaiah 53:5-6 NKJ).

Matthew tells us that *Jesus was wounded and bruised.* "When Pilate saw that he could not prevail at all, but rather that a tumult was rising, he took water and washed his hands before the multitude, saying, 'I am innocent of the blood of this just Person. You see to it.' And all the people answered and said, 'His blood be on us and on our children.' Then he released Barabbas to them; and when he had

188

scourged Jesus, he delivered Him to be crucified" (Matthew 27;24-26 NKJ).

Finally we learn that the *Messiah was to suffer great humiliation by being mocked and despised. King David was speaking of the Messiah when he wrote,* "But I am a worm, and no man; A reproach of men, and despised of the people. All those who see Me laugh Me to scorn; They shoot out the lip, they shake their head, saying, 'He trusted in the LORD, let Him rescue Him, Let Him deliver Him, since He delights in Him' " (Psalms 22:6-8 NKJ)!

Isaiah added these prophetic words, "He is despised and rejected by men, A man of sorrows and acquainted with grief. And we hid, as it were, our faces from Him; He was despised, and we did not esteem Him" (Isaiah 53:3 NKJ).

Looking into the New Testament Scriptures, we learn that *Jesus was humiliated by those who persecuted Him.* Matthew reads, "Then the soldiers of the governor took Jesus into the Praetorium and gathered the whole garrison around Him. And they stripped Him and put a scarlet robe on Him. When they had twisted a crown of thorns, they put it on His head, and a reed in His right hand. And they bowed their knee before Him and mocked Him, saying, 'Hail, King of the Jews!' Then they spat on Him, and took the reed and struck Him on the head. Then when they had mocked Him, they took the robe off Him, put His own clothes on Him, and led Him away to be crucified" (Matthew 27:27-31 NKJ).

C. His Death And Burial

The Hebrew Scriptures foretold many details about the death and burial of the Messiah. Some of these are as follows.

One of the most graphic descriptions foretelling the death of the Messiah is found in the Twenty Second Psalm. David wrote this Psalm about 1,000 years before Jesus was born. In this Psalm, David describes someone being crucified. This is most significant because crucifixion was not the method of capital punishment in David's day. The Jewish method of capital punishment was stoning. It wasn't until the time of the Romans that crucifixion became the common manner of execution. But in this Psalm, David wrote of one being crucified, and he gave much detail about the suffering that would accompany this type of death.

Psalm 22:16 reads, "For dogs have surrounded Me; The assembly of the wicked has enclosed Me. They pierced My hands and My feet" (NKJ).

Zechariah also prophesied of this and wrote, "And someone will say to him, 'What are these wounds in your hands?' Then he will answer, 'Those with which I was wounded in the house of my friends' " (Zechariah 13:6 NKJ).

David spoke of the Messiah having His hands and feet pierced. When someone is crucified, he is placed on the cross by nails that are driven in his hands and feet. This was the type of death that Jesus suffered.

Luke wrote, "Pilate, therefore, wishing to release Jesus, again called out to them. But they shouted saying, 'Crucify Him, crucify Him! And he said to them the third time, 'Why, what evil has he done? I have found no reason for death in Him. I will therefore chastise Him and let Him go.' But they were insistent, demanding with loud voices that He be crucified. And the voices of these men and of the chief priests prevailed. So Pilate gave sentence that it should be as they requested" (Luke 23:20-24 NKJ).

David's statement is such an obvious reference to Jesus that the Jewish scholars translated his words to read, "Like a lion they are at my hands and my feet." This translation is totally out of context with the verse and the chapter. And it was not the translation the Jews used prior to the first coming of Jesus. It was translated this way only after Jesus came because it so clearly pointed to Him as the Messiah.

Isaiah wrote that the Messiah would die with thieves,"
. . . And He was numbered with the transgressors, And He bore the sin of many, And made intercession for the transgressors" (Isaiah 53:12 NKJ).

Matthew recorded that *Jesus was crucified with two thieves.* "Then two robbers were crucified with Him, one on the right and another on the left" (Matthew 27:38 NKJ).

In David's description from Psalm Twenty Two, he added that the Messiah's persecutors would *gamble for His garment.* He said, "They divide My garments among them, And for My clothing they cast lots" (Psalm 22:18 NKJ).

While Jesus was being crucified, the Roman soldiers gambled for His garment. John wrote, "Then the soldiers, when they had crucified Jesus, took His garments and made four parts, to each soldier a part, and also the tunic. Now the tunic was without seam, woven from the top in one piece. They said therefore among themselves, 'Let us not tear it, but cast lots for it, whose it shall be,' that the Scripture might be fulfilled which says: 'They divided My garments among them, And for My clothing they cast lots' " (John 19:23-24 NKJ).

In another Psalm, David wrote that, while being crucified, *the Messiah would acknowledge His thirst and be given vinegar to drink.* Psalm 69:21 reads, "They also gave me gall for my food, And for my thirst they gave me vinegar to drink" (NKJ).

Jesus fulfilled this prophecy just before He died. The apostle John personally saw it all happen and wrote, "After this, Jesus knowing that all things were now accomplished, that the Scripture might be fulfilled, saith, I thirst. Now there was set a vessel full of vinegar: and they filled a sponge with vinegar, and put it upon hyssop, and put it to his mouth. When Jesus had therefore received the vinegar, he said, It is finished: and he bowed his head, and gave up the ghost" (John 19:28-30 KJV).

In David's great Messianic Psalm, he predicted that the *Messiah would be forsaken by God.* David wrote that the Messiah would cry, "My God, My God, why have You forsaken Me. . .?" (Psalm 22:1 NKJ)

These were the same words Jesus spoke from the cross. It was at this moment that He was taking on the sins of mankind. God laid on Jesus the iniquity of us all (Isaiah 53:6) as He became the innocent substitutionary sacrifice for our sins. His words were not a question, but a cry of anguish

191

and distress as He bore our sins and was separated from the eternal fellowship He had with God, the Father.

Matthew recorded this fulfillment of David's prophecy, "And about the ninth hour Jesus cried out with a loud voice saying, 'Eli, Eli, lama sabachtani?' that is, 'My God, My God, why have You forsaken Me' " (Matthew 27:46 NKJ)?

It was also David who told us that during the Messiah's suffering, His bones would not be broken. Psalm 34:20 reads, "He keepeth all his bones: not one of them is broken" (KJV).

When a person is being crucified, his body sags so that he is prevented from getting a full breath of air. In order to overcome this, the person pushes himself up by his heel, takes a deep breath, holds it as long as he can and then sinks down again. In this way, he is able to prolong his life. In view of this, the Roman soldiers would break a person's legs while he was hanging on the cross. This would prevent the person from pushing himself up, thus, hastening his death.

This was the practice of the day when Jesus was crucified. Yet when the Roman soldiers came to break His legs, they did not break them because Jesus was already dead. John was an eyewitness to this and wrote, "Therefore, because it was the Preparation Day, that the bodies should not remain on the cross on the Sabbath (for that Sabbath was a high day), the Jews asked Pilate that their legs might be broken, and that they might be taken away. Then the soldiers came and broke the legs of the first and of the other who was crucified with Him. But when they came to Jesus and saw that He was already dead, they did not break His legs . . . For these things were done that the Scripture might be fulfilled, 'Not one of His bones shall be broken' " (John 19:31-33,36 NKJ).

The prophet Zechariah gave an additional important piece of information about the suffering of the Messiah. He said that the *Messiah would be pierced.* This is in addition to the other prophecy given by David and Zechariah which we just noted. Zechariah said that this pierced Messiah was none other than Jehovah Himself. God spoke the following words through Zechariah concerning the Messiah at His second coming, "And I will pour on the house of David and on the inhabitants of Jerusalem the Spirit of grace and supplication; then they will look upon Me whom they have pierced; they will mourn for Him as one mourns for his only son, and grieve for Him as one grieves for a firstborn" (Zechariah 12:10 NKJ).

While Jesus was hanging on the cross, the Roman soldiers pierced His side. John recorded this happening and said it was a partial fulfillment of Zechariah's prophecy. He wrote, "But one of the soldiers pierced His side with a spear, and immediately blood and water came out. . . And another Scripture says, 'They shall look on Him whom they pierced' " (John 19:34,37 NKJ).

The Hebrew Scriptures were so detailed, they even provided information about the Messiah's burial. Isaiah said that the *Messiah would be buried in a rich man's tomb.* He wrote, "And they made His grave with the wicked—But with the rich at His death. . ." (Isaiah 53:9 NKJ).

Jesus was buried in a rich man's tomb. This rich man was named Joseph of Arimathea. Joseph was a member of the Jewish Supreme Court (the Sanhedrin) which shared the responsibility with Pilate for Jesus' death. But Joseph had become a follower of Jesus and wanted Him to be buried in a dignified manner. So he put Jesus' body in his own tomb.

Matthew wrote, "Now when evening had come, there came a rich man from Arimathea, named Joseph, who himself had also become a disciple of Jesus. This man went to Pilate and asked for the body to be given to him. And when Joseph had taken the body, he wrapped it in a clean linen cloth, and laid it in his new tomb which he had hewn out of the rock; and he rolled a large stone against the door of the tomb, and departed" (Matthew 27:57-60 NKJ).

These are just a few of the many Hebrew Scriptures that predicted the Messiah would have to suffer before entering into His glory. Jesus fulfilled all of them plus many more which we have not considered. Yet, as we've learned, the

Messiah was also to be the Deliverer who would save His people from Gentile domination and establish the golden age about which the prophets spoke. A dead Messiah would not be much of a deliverer. So it was necessary for Jesus to be resurrected and ascend back to heaven from which He came. He would then wait in heaven for a future time when He would come again to planet earth to fulfill the other portrait of Him in the Hebrew Scriptures as the conquering king. Let's now briefly consider some of the Scriptures that give this portrait of the Messiah.

4. The Messiah's Resurrection And Ascension

As we've been learning, David wrote much about the Messiah's suffering. But he also wrote about His resurrection and ascension. David was prophesying these words on behalf of the Messiah when he wrote, "There my heart is glad, and my glory rejoices; My flesh also will rest in hope. For You will not leave my soul in Sheol, Nor will You allow Your Holy One to see corruption" (Psalm 16:9-10 NKJ).

Jesus predicted that He would be killed, yet that He would rise again from the dead after three days. Mark 8:31 reads, "And He began to teach them that the Son of Man must suffer many things, and be rejected by the elders and chief priests and scribes, and be killed, and after three days rise again" (NKJ).

The Jewish leaders who had Jesus put to death remembered His prediction. They were so afraid of Jesus, even after His death, that they persuaded Pilate to assign guards to the place where Jesus was buried until the three days were passed. Roman guards were posted in front of the tomb and secured it with a Roman seal (Matthew 27:62-66).

But all these precautions did not stop David's prophecy from being fulfilled. Three days after Jesus was crucified, He rose from the dead. After His resurrection, an angel came and rolled away the stone that Joseph had placed in front of the tomb. This angel then proclaimed the good news of Jesus' resurrection to some women who had come to mourn at the tomb.

194

Matthew gives the following account of what happened, "Now after the Sabbath, as the first day of the week began to dawn, Mary Magdalene and the other Mary came to see the tomb. And behold, there was a great earthquake; for an angel of the Lord descended from heaven, and came and rolled back the stone from the door, and sat on it. His countenance was like lightning, and his clothing was white as snow. And the guards shook for fear of him and became like dead men. But the angel answered and said to the women, 'Do not be afraid, for I know that you seek Jesus who was crucified. He is not here; for He is risen, as He said. Come, see the place where the Lord lay' " (Matthew 28:1-6 NKJ).

For the next forty days, Jesus appeared to many of His followers. On one occasion, He spoke to a crowd of more than five hundred (1 Corinthians 15:6).

Peter preached that Jesus' resurrection was the fulfillment of David's prophecy. He said, "Men of Israel, hear these words: Jesus of Nazareth, a Man attested by God to you by miracles, wonders, and signs which God did through Him in your midst, as you yourself also know—Him, being delivered by the determined counsel and foreknowledge of God, you have taken by lawless hands, have crucified, and put to death; whom God raised up, having loosed the pains of death, because it was not possible that He should be held by it. For David says concerning Him: 'I foresaw the LORD always before my face, For He is at my right hand, that I may not be shaken; Therefore my heart rejoiced and my tongue was glad; Moreover my flesh will also rest in hope, Because You will not leave my soul in Hades, Nor will You allow Your Holy One to see corruption. You have made known to me the ways of life; You will make me full of joy in Your presence.' Men and brethren, let me speak freely to you of the patriarch David, that he is both dead and buried, and his tomb is with us to this day. Therefore, being a prophet, and knowing that God had sworn with an oath to him that of the fruit of his body, according to the flesh, He would raise up the Christ to sit on his throne, he, foreseeing this, spoke concerning the resurrection of the Christ, that His soul was not left in Hades, nor did His flesh see corruption. This Jesus God has raised up, of which we are all witnesses" (Acts 2:22-32 NKJ).

David also had the blessing of predicting the Messiah's ascension to heaven and ultimate rule. He wrote, "THE LORD said to my Lord, 'Sit at My right hand, Till I make Your enemies Your footstool' (Psalm 110:1 NKJ).

After Jesus was resurrected, His followers thought that He would immediately overthrow the Romans and restore the kingdom of David. But as we've learned, this was not to take place until the end of a long period of time in which the Gentiles would be given an opportunity to acknowledge Jesus as their personal Lord and Savior. As we study the Scriptures and look back into history, we see that this time period was to be 2,000 years.

The book of Acts tells us of the ascension with these words, "Now when He (Jesus) had spoken these things, while they watched, He was taken up, and a cloud received Him out of their sight. And while they looked steadfastly toward heaven as He went up, behold two men stood by them in white apparal, who also said, 'Men of Galilee, why do you stand gazing up into heaven? This same Jesus, who was taken up from you into heaven, will so come in like manner as you saw Him go into heaven' " (Acts 1:9-11 NKJ).

In Peter's sermon, he went on to point out that Jesus was not only resurrected, but that He also had ascended to heaven to sit at the right hand of God, the Father, in fulfillment of David's prophecy. Peter preached, "This Jesus has God raised up, of which we are all witnesses. Therefore being exalted to the right hand of God, and having received from the Father the promise of the Holy Spirit, He poured out this which you now see and hear. For David did not ascend into the heavens, but he says himself: 'The LORD said to my Lord, 'Sit at My right hand, Till I make Your enemies Your footstool.' Therefore let all the house of Israel know assuredly that God has made this Jesus, whom you crucified, both Lord and Christ" (Acts 2:32-36 NKJ).

5. The Messiah's Coming In Power And Glory

Finally, the Hebrew Scriptures spoke about the second coming of the Messiah in power and glory. Some of these Scriptures and their New Testament fulfillment in Jesus are listed below.

"Yet I have set My King On My holy hill of Zion.

I will declare the decree: The LORD has said to Me, 'You are My son. Today I have begotten You. Ask of Me, and I will give You the nations for your inheritance, And the ends of the earth for your possession. You shall break them with a rod of iron; You shall dash them in pieces like a potter's vessel.'

Now therefore, be wise, O kings; Be instructed, you judges of the earth. Serve the LORD with fear, And rejoice with trembling. Kiss the son, lest He be angry, And you perish in the way, When His wrath is kindled but a little. Blessed are all those who put their trust in Him" (Psalm 2:6-12 NKJ).

"For unto us a child is born, Unto us a son is given: and the government shall be upon his shoulder: and his name shall be called Wonderful, Counsellor, The mighty God, The everlasting Father, The Prince of Peace. Of the increase of his government and peace there shall be no end, upon the throne of David, and upon his kingdom, to order it, and to establish it with judgement and with justice from henceforth even forever. The zeal of the LORD of hosts will perform this (Isaiah 9:6-7 KJV).

And in the days of these kings the God of heaven will set up a kingdom which shall never be destroyed; and the kingdom shall not be left to other people; it shall break in pieces and consume all these kingdoms, and it shall stand forever" (Daniel 2:44 NKJ).

"I was watching in the night visions, And behold One like the Son of Man, Coming with the clouds of heaven! He came to the Ancient of Days, and they brought Him

197

near before Him. Then to him was given dominion and glory and a kingdom, That all peoples, nations, and languages should serve Him. His dominion is an everlasting dominion, Which shall not pass away, And His kingdom the one Which shall not be destroyed" (Daniel 7:13-14 NKJ).

"Then the kingdom and dominion, And the greatness of the kingdoms under the whole heaven, Shall be given to the people, the saints of the Most High. His kingdom is an everlasting kingdom, And all dominions shall serve and obey Him" (Daniel 7:27 NKJ).

"Then the LORD will go forth And fight against the nations, As He fights in the day of battle. And in that day His feet will stand on the Mount of Olives, Which faces Jerusalem on the east. And the Mount of Olives shall be split in two From east to west, Making a very large valley; Half of the mountain shall move toward the north And half of it toward the south . . .Thus the LORD my God will come, And all the saints with You. . . And the LORD shall be King over all the earth. In that day it shall be—'The LORD is one,' And His name one" (Zechariah 14:3-5,9 NKJ).

"Then I saw heaven opened, and behold a white horse. And He who sat on him was called Faithful and True, and in righteousness he judges and makes war. His eyes were like a flame of fire, and on His head were many crowns. He had a name written that no one knew except Himself. He was clothed with a robe dipped in blood, and His name is called The Word of God. And the armies in heaven, clothed in fine linen, white and clean, followed Him on white horses. Now out of His mouth goes a sharp sword, that with it He should strike the nations. And He Himself will rule them with a rod of iron. He Himself treads the winepress of the fierceness and wrath of Almighty God. And He has on His robe and on His thigh a name written: KING OF

KINGS AND LORD OF LORDS" (Revelation 19:11-16 NKJ).

Isaiah yearned for God to come and establish His kingdom. Isaiah's heart cried out to God, "Oh, that you would rend the heavens! That You would come down! That the mountains might shake at Your presence" (Isaiah 64:1 NKJ).

The apostle John concluded the book of Revelation with the same heart cry. John said, "Even so, come Lord Jesus" (Revelation 22:20 NKJ).

Dear reader, are you ready for the coming of the Messiah?

Maranatha! Shalom!

HOW TO RECOGNIZE THE JEWISH MESSIAH

1. The Messiah's Birth
   A. Place of birth (Mic. 5:2; Mat. 2:1)
   B. Manner of birth (Is. 7:14; Lk. 1:26-35)
   C. Time of birth (Gen. 49:10; Lk. 21:24)
   D. Ancestry (1 Chr. 17:11-14; Lk. 1:31-33)
2. Messiah's Life and Ministry
   A. Herald by Forerunner (Is. 40:3; Mal. 3:1; Mat. 3:1-3)
   B. Ministry to poor and needy (Is. 61:1-2; Lk. 4:16-21)
   C. Worker of Miracles (Is. 35:4-6; Mat. 11:1-6)
   D. Acknowledged by many (Zech. 9:9; Mat. 21:4-9)
   E. Rejected by most (Is. 53:3; Mat. 27:15-26)
3. Messiah's Suffering
   A. His Betrayal
      1. Betrayed by a friend (Ps. 41:9; Jn. 13:18,21,26)
      2. For 30 pieces of silver (Zech. 11:12; Mat. 26:14-26)
      3. Silver cast down in temple (Zech. 11:13; Mat. 27:3-7)
   B. His Trials
      1. Falsely accused (Ps. 35:11-12; Mat. 26:59-60)
      2. Silent before accusers (Is. 53:7; Mat. 27:12-14)
      3. Smitten and spat on (Is. 50:6; 53:4-8; Mic. 5:1; Mat. 26:67)
      4. Wounded and bruised (Is. 53:5-6; Mat. 27:24-26)
      5. Mocked and despised (Ps. 22:6-8; Is. 53:3; Mat. 27:27-31)
   C. His Death and Burial
      1. Hands and feet pierced (Ps. 22:16; Zech. 13:6; Lk. 23:20-24)
      2. Crucified with thieves (Is. 53:12; Mat. 27:38)
      3. Garment parted/lot cast (Ps. 22:18; Jn. 19:23-24)
      4. Given gall and vinegar (Ps. 69:21; Jn. 19:28-30)
      5. Forsaken by God (Ps. 22:1; Mat. 27:46)
      6. Not a bone broken (Ps. 34:20; Jn. 19:31-33,36)
      7. Side pierced (Zech. 12:10; Jn. 19:34,37)
      8. Buried with rich (Is. 53:9; Mat. 27:57-60)
4. Messiah's Resurrection and Ascension
   A. His Resurrection (Ps. 16:10; Mat. 28:1-6; Acts 2:22-32)
   B. His ascension (Ps. 110:1-2; Acts 1:9-11; 2:32-36)
5. Messiah's Coming in Power and Glory
   A. His Second Coming (Zech. 14:3-4,9; Rev. 19:11-16)
   B. His Universal Rule (Ps. 2:6-12; Rev. 20:1-6)

Chapter 16—How To Recognize The Jewish Messiah

Study Guide 15

1. Briefly describe the two portraits of the Messiah presented in the Hebrew Scriptures.

   Political - Powerful Ruler.
   Religious - Lowley Servant Sufferer.

2. Explain what is meant by the phrase "Messianic tunnel vision" and describe how the Jews came to be blinded by it. *It was taught that the only Messiah was the powerful Messiah to come. They neglected the Religious suffering Messiah*

3. State the relationship between the Hebrew Scriptures and Jesus of Nazareth.

   They are related and fulfilled.

BIBLE STUDY MATERIALS BY RICHARD BOOKER

BOOKS
For additional copies of this or other books by Richard Booker, order through your local bookstore or clip and mail the Order Form which is provided on the last page of this book following the tape list.

THE MIRACLE OF THE SCARLET THREAD
This book explains how the Old and New Testaments are woven together by the scarlet thread of the blood covenant to tell one complete story throughout the Bible.

COME AND DINE
This book takes the mystery and confusion out of the Bible. It provides background information on how we got the Bible, a survey of every book in the Bible and how each relates to Jesus Christ, practical principles, forms and guidelines for your own personal Bible study and a systematic plan for effectively reading, studying and understanding the Bible for yourself.

INTIMACY WITH GOD
This book is about the God of the Bible. It shows the ways in which God has revealed Himself to us and explains the attributes, plans and purposes of God. Then each attribute is related practically to the reader. This book takes you into the very heart of God and demonstrates how to draw near to Him.

RADICAL CHRISTIAN LIVING
This book explains how you can grow to become a mature Christian and help others do so as well. You'll learn the pathway to Christian maturity and how to select and train others in personal follow-up and disciplining at different levels of Christian growth.

SEATED IN HEAVENLY PLACES

This book helps the reader learn how to live the victorious Christian life and walk in the power of God. It explains how to minister to others, wear the armor of God and exercise spiritual authority.

BLOW THE TRUMPET IN ZION

This book explains the dramatic story of God's covenant plan for Israel including their past glory and suffering, present crisis and future hope.

CHRISTIAN GROWTH SEMINARS

COME AND DINE

This is a one-day workshop designed for the purpose of teaching people how to study the Bible for themselves systematically. Each participant receives a 96-page workbook.

HOW TO GET YOUR PRAYERS ANSWERED

This is a one-day seminar designed for the purpose of helping Christians learn how to pray more effective and powerful prayers that will get positive results. Each participant receives an 84-page workbook.

AUDIO CASSETTE TAPE ALBUMS

A list of Richard's teaching cassettes is included on the following pages. All tape series come in an attractive album for your convenience. To order tapes, check the appropriate box, then clip and mail the Order Form which is provided on the last page of this book following the tape list.

TAPE LIST

■ The Bible Series
BL1   Uniqueness Of The Bible
BL2   How The Books Became The Book
BL3   Survey of Old Testament
BL4   Survey of New Testament
BL5   How We Got Our English Bible
BL6   Getting Into The Bible
BL7   How To Study The Bible
BL8   How To Understand The Bible

■ Getting To Know God—1
KG1   Knowing God
KG2   The Self-Existing One
KG3   The Personal Spirit
KG4   The Trinity

■ Getting To Know God—2
KG1   God Is Sovereign
KG2   God Is All Power
KG3   God is All Knowledge
KG4   God is Everywhere Present
KG5   God Never Changes

■ Getting to Know God—3
KG1   God Is Holy
KG2   God Is Love
KG3   God Is Just
KG4   God Is Good

■ Blood Covenant Series
BC1   The Blood Covenant
BC2   What Was It Abraham Believed
BC3   The Tabernacle
BC4   The Sacrifices
BC5   The High Priest
BC6   The Passover

■ Abundant Life Series
AL1   Knowing Your Dominion
AL2   Identifying With Christ
AL3   Appropriating His Lordship
AL4   Walking in the Spirit
AL5   Ministering in the Spirit
AL6   Wearing the Armor

■ The Church Series
CH1   The Church
CH2   The Body of Christ
CH3   Gifts of the Spirit
CH4   Equipping the Saints
CH5   Work of the Ministry
CH6   Building Up the Body

■ Christian Family Series
CF1   God's Purpose for Family
CF2   The Husband's Role
CF3   The Wife's Role
CF4   Parent & Children Roles

■ Faith & Healing Series
FH1   Divine Healing Today
FH2   Basis for Claiming Healing
FH3   Barriers To Healing

■ End Time Series
ET1   Coming World Events—1
ET2   Coming World Events—2
ET3   Judgment Of Christians
ET4   Seven-Year Tribulation
ET5   Second Coming of Christ
ET6   Millennium
ET7   Great White Throne Judgment
ET8   New Heaven & New Earth

■ The Feasts Series
FE1   Passover
FE2   Unleavened Bread
FE3   Pentecost
FE4   Trumpets
FE5   Atonement
FE6   Tabernacles

■ Sacrifices Series
SF1   Sin Offering
SF2   Trespass Offering
SF3   Burnt Offering
SF4   Meal Offering
SF5   Peace Offering

■ *Get Your Prayers Answered*

PR1 Intruduction To Prayer
PR2 Principles of Prayer
PR3 Why Prayers Aren't Answered
PR4 Persistence In Prayer
PR5 Intercessory Prayer
PR6 Fasting And Prayer

■ *Ephesians Series*

EP1 Background & Blessing
EP2 Prayer For Enlightenment
EP3 New Life In Christ
EP4 Who Is The Seed Of Abraham
EP5 Prayer For Enablement
EP6 Christian Unity
EP7 Ministering To The Saints
EP8 Ministry Of The Saints
EP9 Shedding The Graveclothes
EP10 Initiating The Father
EP11 God's Order For Family
EP12 Spiritual Warfare

■ *Phillipians Series*

PH1 Background & Prayer
PH2 Victory In Tribulation
PH3 Keys To Unity
PH4 Honoring One Another
PH5 True Righteousness
PH6 Going On With God
PH7 Standing Together
PH8 Sufficiency Of God

■ *Colossians Series*

CO1 Background
CO2 Person & Work Of Christ
CO3 Christ In You
CO4 Sufficiency Of Christ
CO5 Christ Our Life
CO6 New Man In Christ
CO7 Christ In The Home
CO8 Christ Outside The Home

■ *Thessalonians Series*

TH1 Background & Prayer
TH2 A Winning Defense
TH3 A Welcome Report
TH4 Walking to Please God
TH5 The Day of the Lord
TH6 Background & Prayer
TH7 Day of the Lord Again
TH8 No Bums Allowed

■ *Practical Studies—1*

PS1 Living By Faith
PS2 Guidance
PS3 Prayer
PS4 Fasting
PS5 Meditation
PS6 Stewardship

■ *Single Messages (Circle Below)*

SM1 Why God Had To Become Man
SM2 Who Was That God Begat
SM3 Feasts Of The Lord
SM4 Philemon
SM5 Lord's Prayer
SM6 Handling Worry
SM7 Knowing God's Will
SM8 Spiritual Leprosy
SM9 Praying In The Name
SM10 Bible Baptisms
SM11 Signs Of His Coming
SM12 Times Of The Gentiles
SM13 Christian Giving
SM14 Master Theme Of Bible
SM15 The Dominant Force
SM16 Personal Testimony
SM17 Call To Discipleship
SM18 Where Are the Dead?

■ *Foundational Studies—1*

FS1 Knowing the Bible
FS2 Knowing God
FS3 Knowing Jesus Christ
FS4 Knowing the Holy Spirit
FS5 Knowing Man
FS6 Knowing the Enemy

■ *Foundational Studies—2*

FS1 Living the Abundant Life
FS2 Water Baptism
FS3 Communion
FS4 Nature of the church
FS5 The End Times
FS6 Life After Death

■ *Practical Studies—2*

PS1 Handling Trials
PS2 Sharing your faith
PS3 Worship
PS4 Praise
PS5 Health and Healing
PS6 Family Life

BOOK ORDER FORM

Ordering Instructions
To order books, check the appropriate box, then clip and mail the coupon below to **SOUNDS OF THE TRUMPET, INC., 8230 BIRCHGLENN, HOUSTON, TX 77070.**

. . . .

☐ Please send me ____ copy(ies) of THE MIRACLE OF THE SCARLET THREAD. I have enclosed $4.95 contribution for each copy ordered (No C.O.D.), plus $1.00 for mailing.

☐ Please send me ____ copy(ies) of COME AND DINE. I have enclosed a $5.95 contribution for each copy ordered (No C.O.D.), plus $1.00 for mailing.

☐ Please send me ____ copy(ies) of INTIMACY WITH GOD. I have enclosed a $5.95 contribution for each copy ordered (No C.O.D.), plus $1.00 for mailing.

☐ Please send me ____ copy(ies) of RADICAL CHRISTIAN LIVING. I have enclosed a $4.95 contribution for each copy ordered plus $1.00 for mailing.

☐ Please send me ____ copy(ies) of SEATED IN HEAVENLY PLACES at $4.95 per copy plus $1.00 for mailing.

☐ Please send me ____ copy(ies) of BLOW THE TRUMPET IN ZION at $5.95 per copy plus $1.00 for mailing.

Name _____
Street _____
City _____
State _____ ZIP _____

TAPE ORDER FORM

Ordering Instructions
To order tapes, check the appropriate box, then clip and mail the coupon below to SOUNDS OF THE TRUMPET, INC., 8230 BIRCHGLENN, HOUSTON, TX 77070.

. . . .

☐ Please send me the following tapes. I have enclosed a $4.00 contribution for each tape ordered (No C.O.D.), plus $1.00 for mailing

☐ The Bible Series	($32.00)	☐ The Feasts Series	($24.00)
☐ Getting To Know God—1	($16.00)	☐ The Sacrifices Series	($20.00)
☐ Getting To Know God—2	($20.00)	☐ Love Notes From Jesus	($28.00)
☐ Getting To Know God—3	($16.00)	☐ Ephesians Series	($48.00)
☐ Blood Covenant Series	($24.00)	☐ Philippians Series	($32.00)
☐ Abundant Life Series	($24.00)	☐ Colossians Series	($32.00)
☐ The Church Series	($24.00)	☐ Thessalonians Series	($32.00)
☐ The Christian Family	($16.00)	☐ Single Messages (Circle)	
☐ Faith & Healing Series	($12.00)	(SM1,2,3,4,5,6,7,8,9,10,	($4.00 each)
☐ End Times Series	($32.00)	11,12,13,14,15,16,17,18)	
☐ Prayer Series	($24.00)	☐ Practical Studies—1	($24.00)
☐ Foundational Studies—1	($24.00)	☐ Practical Studies—2	($24.00)
☐ Foundational Studies—2	($24.00)		

Name _____

Street _____

City _____

State _____ ZIP _____